EDITED BY KRISTIN FEIREISS AND LUKAS FEIREISS

ARCHITECTURE OF CHANGE 2

SUSTAINABILITY AND HUMANITY IN THE BUILT ENVIRONMENT

CONTENTS

DUTY OF CARE

Unfolding Tomorrow – Thriving for Fictions
of Our Multiple Futures
Lukas Feireiss in Conversation
with Chris Luebkeman
Part 1

TOMORROW NEVER DIES

Unfolding Tomorrow – Thriving for Fictions
of Our Multiple Futures
Lukas Feireiss in Conversation
with Chris Luebkeman
Part 2

CHANGE / BY

KRISTIN FEIREISS

One thing is certain: environmental sustainability, as an issue of far-reaching global significance, has created unprecedented consensus between public and political opinion. Its role as an issue in all areas of society and political discourse is continually growing. For those working in the field of sustainability, it is as if all doors have suddenly been opened. Indeed, where there is no longer resistance, sustainable attitudes to everyday life can become the norm. That said, there is consensus amongst scientists and experts that we are still only in the early stages of testing and developing sustainable strategies for the future.

Current figures back this up quite clearly: construction and the urban environment are responsible for the consumption of a significant proportion of our natural resources, for one third of energy consumption, for 30 to 40 per cent of emissions, and for as much as 50 to 60 per cent of mass waste production. These are facts that had already been established over 30 years ago in the first Club of Rome report, and their continued validity has only been confirmed and more precisely defined by recent United Nations reports.

To quote Werner Sobek: "Now that we have generally recognised our responsibility to future generations, there is no longer any doubt that we cannot continue to behave as we have." Urban planners, architects and engineers have a significant role to play in dealing with the problems facing us and in developing and testing sustainable solutions.

With diverse efforts being made in this field, there is a danger that sustainability will be treated principally as a quantitative issue, where only energy and resource consumption is considered and qualitative aspects are neglected or ignored. If architects really want to address sustainability responsibly, then cultural, topographical and geopolitical contexts must be considered alongside climate issues. According to Stefan Behnisch, in order to remain in harmony with our natural environment, we must reconsider the means and methods with which we construct every building in every corner of the earth: "Only once we have established how to deal with this issue can sustainability take its place among the many other architectural disciplines, no longer standing in the foreground of design but rather integrating with the other disciplines."

There is no doubt that we still have a long way to go. The demands of three renowned architects and experts in this field clearly illustrate the spectrum of approaches that can be taken. For Stefan Behnisch, the most important prerequisite for sustainable construction is to realise that buildings are not just machines to be geared for the highest possible efficiency; above all else, buildings have been and will remain humanity's most important cultural artefacts.

With the striking and illustrative motto "From Bauhaus to Treehouse", Michael Braungardt identifies his approach: away from the tabula rasa of modernism in favour of house designs that actively help to recreate nature. At the same time, the goal is not to romanticise of nature, but rather to create as equal a partnership as possible.

And finally, Werner Sobek, who correctly identifies and regrets the lack of a risk-taking culture worldwide, calls for more courage in experimenting and implementing prototypes with the aim of creating a more liveable environment, as this is the only way to fulfil new targets.

Many of these wishes, hopes and expectations can be found in this publication – the second volume in the series *Architecture of Change* – in the form of imaginative, fascinating and innovative research projects as well as constructed buildings addressing sustainability from the last two years – from Foreign Office Architects' Meydan Retail Complex in Turkey to Renzo Piano's California Academy of Science in San Francisco to OMA's masterplan for the North Sea. All these works respond to various societal, cultural, economic and climatic conditions in different regions of the world.

As in the first *Architecture of Change* book, the 40 projects presented here are the result of a year of intensive research for the Zumtobel Group Award 2009. They represent works chosen from a total of around 200 assembled by Lukas Feireiss and Sophie Lovell with the help of an international team of experts including architects and architecture critics Leon van Schaick (Australia), Erwin Viray (Singapore) and Friedrich von Borries (Germany).

The Zumtobel Group Award for Sustainability and Humanity in the Built Environment was not awarded in 2009 due to the current financial crisis. However, with this publication, Zumtobel demonstrates its ongoing commitment to pursue the aims of the awards in its corporate philosophy, wishing also to publicise the selected projects. With determination, *Architecture of Change 2* contributes in tackling the challenges of integrated approaches to sustainability. ◤

BUILDING UP RESPONSIBILITY IN CRITICAL TIMES / BY LUKAS FEIREISS

THE TIMES THEY ARE A-CHANGIN'

»LIFE BELONGS TO THE LIVING, AND HE WHO LIVES MUST BE PREPARED FOR CHANGES.«

Johann Wolfgang von Goethe

What turbulent times we are living in! Only one and a half years ago, when we edited the first *Architecture of Change* book as an interdisciplinary source of inspiration for the discussion of sustainable approaches within the built environment, the topic of climate change was on everyone's lips. A sudden global alarmism about the vulnerability of our planet was spreading across all fields of knowledge and experience. From politics to pop, from the mainstream to the avant-garde, a new rhetoric was coined by an urgent demand for change. Change itself even became the slogan and synonym for a historic election campaign in the United States. An anthem of hope spread across the globe. But with the subsequent rock-bottom financial crash of the global banking sector, only the headlines changed and the subject of global warming was put on hold. Certainly, mere environmental disasters are far less important than a world economic crisis in a global society that is driven by monetary values. And now, at the moment of writing, we have come somewhat to terms with the inevitability of a worldwide economic depression and a highly aggressive influenza virus dispersed across the globe, keeping the world's population agitated. Welcome to the global village! All of these examples are sole expressions of the apparent lessening or elimination of barriers and the increased cross-border flows of literally everything from goods to services, and from people to capital and culture and even diseases that characterise today's globalised world. It is a sign of the times, a stamp of globalisation, that events – no matter how small or local they might be – have the power to exert immediate and far-reaching global effects. It is not only against the backdrop of the latest financial crisis that this system displays obvious epidemic qualities, being unable to regulate itself. It is surely not too far fetched even to compare the collapse of the banking industry to a viral infection that is spread from one bank to another, which accounts for increasing numbers of casualties over a certain period of incubation. American novelist Gore Vidal once compared the earth to "a living organism that is being attacked by billions of bacteria whose numbers double every 40 years". His conclusion was that either the host dies, or the virus dies, or both. I do not think we need to conform fully to this extreme comparison to understand that we act in concert. We are sitting in the same boat: globalisation not only means shared vulnerability but also common responsibility – no matter what crisis will rule the headlines by the time this book is published. ◢

IT ALL COMES DOWN TO THE GREEN

»A DOCTOR CAN BURY HIS MISTAKES, BUT AN ARCHITECT CAN ONLY ADVISE HIS CLIENTS TO PLANT VINES.«

Frank Lloyd Wright

Today this cynical comment on the limits of architectural problem-solving, by one of the undisputed godfathers of modern architecture, reminds us not only of the irrevocable factuality of the built building, for good or for bad, but also of green-washing practices established in recent years in the field of architecture. Green building and sustainable architecture have been easily manipulated by architects, whose success hinges on publicity. According to Dutch architect Rem Koolhaas, the ecological promise has even become the obligatory ornament of contemporary building practices. *Volume Magazine* recently called sustainability "the magic S-word" that seems to point to a universal idea, valid anywhere, at any time. But whether we call it an environmental imperative, a political issue, a technical challenge, or even the all-encompassing formula for saving the world, it is clear that no simple, quick solution will solve the problem, as the issue at hand is far too complex. Nevertheless, in an urban millennium, in which cities produce 75 per cent of CO_2 emissions, the battle for the future will very probably be decided on urban terrain. It is therefore neither wrong nor naive to believe that it is actually the city planners, architects and engineers who will take over the role of world saviours - given that the respective clients and contractors play along. The oft-repeated statistics to prove this assumption are numerous: today the construction and maintenance of buildings are the largest source of carbon emissions and account for approximately half of the world's total emissions; worldwide, one third of energy consumption is used for the heating or cooling of buildings; etc. Simply speaking: the problem must be tackled, solutions must be discussed, but at least we do not need to argue any longer whether the problem truly exists. ◤

PUSH THINGS FORWARD

»LEARN FROM YESTERDAY, LIVE FOR TODAY, HOPE FOR TOMORROW. THE IMPORTANT THING IS NOT TO STOP QUESTIONING.«

Albert Einstein

Like its predecessor, this volume introduces innovative examples of architecture and engineering, as well as proactive research projects, that address the challenges of environmental friendliness in the built environment through the combination of creativity, scientific insight, technological innovation, commitment to society and social responsibility. At the same time, it critically discusses associated questions with internationally acclaimed experts from the worlds of architecture, art, science and philosophy. The German philosopher Peter

Sloterdijk has been engaged in the fundamental discussion of architecture, space and nature in the making of this book, as well as Chris Luebkeman, Director of the Global Foresight, Incubation and Innovation initiative at Arup. Thanks is also due to Icelandic-born artist Olafur Eliasson, whose work frames the book. *Architecture of Change* is about the convergence of creativity and innovation and of theory and practice, where invention, performance, aesthetics and a deep knowledge of the human factor combine to create experimental approaches and designs. About 40 projects are presented in this book under four intergradient thematic headings to create a novel image of sustainable thinking and action that opens up a representative perspective on the current state of development in this field. The projects, however, remain essentially open, even inviting exchanges of ideas. After all, we believe that the fundamental role of the architect is to translate scientific and technological revolutions into approachable environments that can change people's lives. In this way, the solutions should not only solve but also resonate with the complex problems out of which they have arisen. ◄

AFTER THE CRISIS

»REALITY LEAVES A LOT TO THE IMAGINATION.«

John Lennon

01 140-metre-high Greenpeace banner in the financial district of Frankfurt/Main, Germany, in spring 2009: "If the world were a bank, you would have saved it long ago!"

With the United Nations Climate Change Conference in Copenhagen ahead of us, 2009 is a critical year for all climate activists. We will soon understand the urgency of the ecological crisis facing us and how much will actively need to be done to stop it. A follow-up contract to succeed the Kyoto Protocol in 2013 is to be decided in Copenhagen, the results of which will largely affect the world of tomorrow. Against this backdrop, this book tries to offer a versatile approach to the timely discussion of ecological building practices and participatory approaches within the fields of architecture and engineering – a discussion that is fluid in its scale and disciplinary approach. It is clear to us that this is not an easy road to pursue. But if there is no struggle, there is no progress either. After all, a crisis describes not only a time of intense difficulty and trouble but also an opportunity, a turning point when an important change takes place. Literally speaking, a crisis (from the Greek noun *krisis* = decision) calls for a decision; it is the decisive moment that determines the outcome of the plot, one that indicates either recovery or death. ◄

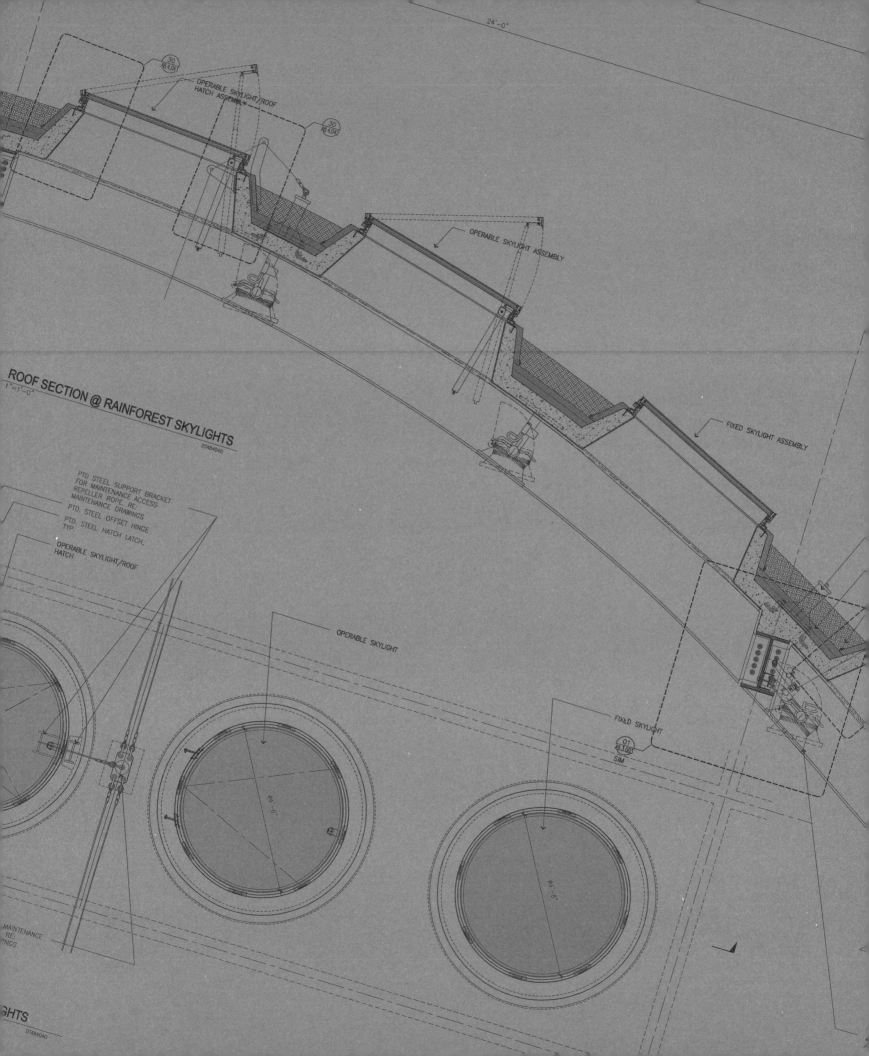

24'-0"

OPERABLE SKYLIGHT/ROOF
HATCH ASSEMBLY

OPERABLE SKYLIGHT ASSEMBLY

ROOF SECTION @ RAINFOREST SKYLIGHTS
1"=1'-0"

D7A84040

FIXED SKYLIGHT ASSEMBLY

PTD STEEL SUPPORT BRACKET
FOR MAINTENANCE ACCESS
REPELLER ROPE. RE:
MAINTENANCE DRAWINGS
PTD. STEEL OFFSET HINGE
PTD. STEEL HATCH LATCH.
TYP.
OPERABLE SKYLIGHT/ROOF
HATCH

OPERABLE SKYLIGHT

FIXED SKYLIGHT

01
A9.1.003
SIM

Ø4'-6"

Ø4'-6"

MAINTENANCE
RE:
NGS

GHTS

D7A84040

CAN I GET A WITNESS

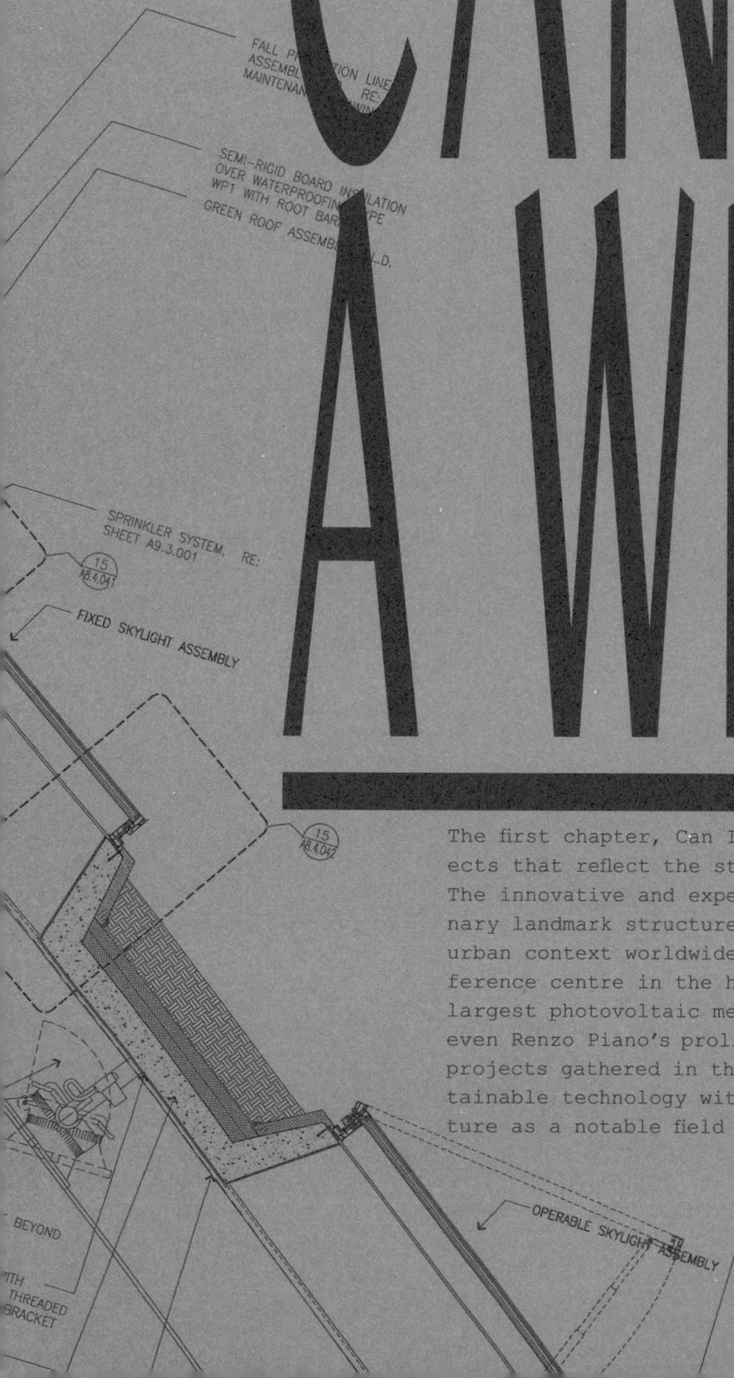

The first chapter, Can I Get a Witness, looks at outstanding architectonic projects that reflect the state of the art in sustainable building practices today. The innovative and experimental uses of technology presented in these extraordinary landmark structures define new standards in sustainable building within the urban context worldwide. Whether it be the new design of a convention and conference centre in the heart of Berlin by Swiss-based architects E2A, the world's largest photovoltaic media wall by Simone Giostra and Partners in Beijing, or even Renzo Piano's prolific California Academy of Sciences in San Francisco, the projects gathered in this chapter raise global interest in the integration of sustainable technology within architecture and reinforce the reputation of architecture as a notable field for discussing and implementing of future developments.

FALL PROTECTION LINE
ASSEMBLY, RE:
MAINTENANCE MANUAL.

SEMI-RIGID BOARD INSULATION
OVER WATERPROOFING TYPE
WP1 WITH ROOT BARRIER.
GREEN ROOF ASSEMBLY, U.N.O.

SPRINKLER SYSTEM, RE:
SHEET A9.3.001

15
A8.4.041

FIXED SKYLIGHT ASSEMBLY.

15
A8.4.042

BEYOND

WITH
THREADED
BRACKET

OPERABLE SKYLIGHT ASSEMBLY

LUKAS FEIREISS IN CONVERSATION WITH PETER SLOTERDIJK PART I

DYNAMIC DWEL- LING IN THE AGE OF FIREWORKS

Peter Sloterdijk (b. 1947) is one of the most prominent German-speaking philosophers today. His works number among the best-selling philosophical books of the twentieth century. Sloterdijk is Professor for Aesthetics and Philosophy and Rector at the Staatliche Hochschule für Gestaltung Karlsruhe.

LF: Mr. Sloterdijk, you regularly participate in debates on architectural theory as a philosopher and cultural theorist. That may be in part because, in your monumental trilogy *Sphären* (Spheres) – *Blasen* (Bubbles), *Globen* (Globes), and *Schäume* (Foams) – you have made space a central category of your theory concerning the life-world. In that three-volume cultural history of space, you characterise man as a container maker who creates the space in which he lives. What is the source of your interest in the interpretation of space for cultural theory?

PS: I belong to the tradition of phenomenological-anthropological theorists inspired by Martin Heidegger, who described man as first and foremost a dwelling animal. In my case, dwelling is only relevant in the form of dynamic dwelling: I emphasise the partially visible, partially invisible dynamic of moving that is always inherent in dwelling. That is one of the differences between my work and that of earlier theorists of space, for whom concepts such as disquiet and security play an important role – to recall Otto Friedrich Bollnow's book *Unruhe und Geborgenheit im Weltbild neuerer Dichter* (Disquiet and security in the worldview of modern poets), which was very famous at the time. My interest in space started with the basic anthropological supposition that man is by nature a changer of milieus. Changes in milieu become existentially significant when someone in a given milieu has constant memories of another one, who brings along a previous milieu, like the exile who retains the old homeland in his new one. Over time, it became clear to me that we need to develop a general anthropology of exile. In that context, architecture becomes important. My idea is that all houses are places of asylum – containers for people who cannot entirely forget that they once lived somewhere else. Their current house is never the first container but always the second or third one, and so on. One moves into a house by changing houses; one furnishes it as a new arrival, as a refugee, or as someone from somewhere else. This motif of changing milieu is the basis of my interest in space.

At the same time, I developed a second approach to the subject of space. Very early on, I encountered the phenomenon that houses and architectural structures in general represent something like immune systems in spatial form. For some time, I have been working on the idea that traditional forms of metaphysics – including so-called religions, ethical systems and value systems – all have to be reformulated in terms of a general immunology. To put it simply, man is a creature that cannot live without means of protection. He needs protection because he feels more threatened by openness to the world and to events than any other living creature does. To assert themselves in the space of experiences that is our world, people prepare themselves in advance for what might confront them – that is what constitutes the principle of immunity. Immunological structures are the embodiments of expectations of injury, damage, and disadvantages – and, in this context, the question of architecture inevitably arises. Already the oldest references to people placing barriers between themselves and their surroundings reveal a primordial interest in protection. There are very old archaeological finds from Africa, probably more than a million years old, that recall something like primitive textile walls. Indeed, stones were found lined up on the ground in an odd manner, and their position only makes sense if they are explained as a way to hold palm fronds in the ground, as a kind of windbreak. As far as I know, this is the oldest indication of an active climate modification by hominoids. It was thus the first attempt to structure our relationship to the world by means of a wall: evidently, a different climate was supposed to prevail inside the wall than did outside it. It is a primitive sketch for a difference between inside and outside expressed in architecture. We shouldn't forget this when we talk about architectural theory in general. The crucial thing is that the person who wishes to dwell will take up a position on the protected side of the wall. That marks the beginning of the shared history of people and walls. ◣

MY INTEREST IN SPACE STARTED WITH THE BASIC ANTHROPOLOGICAL SUPPOSITION THAT MAN IS BY NATURE A CHANGER OF MILIEUS.

HOUSES AND ARCHITECTURAL STRUCTURES IN GENERAL REPRESENT SOMETHING LIKE IMMUNE SYSTEMS IN SPATIAL FORM

LF: You describe the mastery of edges and boundaries as the immunological meaning of building cities and the world, without which we can neither live nor think. The built environment has always been demarcated from its counterpart, the natural environment. The fundamental goal of architecture from the outset has been to provide man with shelter and protection from a broad variety of risks and threats. Architecture is thus always a defence mechanism. In a way, architecture, as the practice of creating autonomous environments, stands in opposition to the nature that surrounds it. To press the point, does architecture need this basic confrontational constellation in order to establish itself?

PS: It's not just so-called outside nature we shield ourselves from! The wall does not simply produce a cosmic outside but also a social and political one. That is most evident from the large walls of the ancient world, those heroic major architectural projects that unmistakably served to keep the enemy outside. To my mind, the point is to make the problem of inside/outside a theme, using the means of a general cultural history. In essence, however, you are right. Initially, architecture exists only to the extent that people use their buildings as protected sites. Naturally, even early on, certain types of architecture did not evince such an overwhelming human connection — sacred architecture, for example, does not make us feel at home but rather alienates us. By means of the templum effect, the sacred space is distinguished from the continuum of the profane. This results in another, inhuman or superhuman approach to the problem of space. The human approach is unmistakably connected to the dialectic of inside and outside. The architects active on that front interpret man as a being who needs an interior and creates an interior. ▸

LF: Should the tension between inside and outside you are describing be equated with the classical conflict of nature versus culture? By that I mean tracing the concept of culture back to its prosaic origin in the cultivation of arable land, as opposed to the nature growing wild around it.

PS: The antithesis of culture and nature alone won't get us very far. In the history of architecture in the stricter sense, people have always been interested in integrating the so-called outside world into the human zone. You see that in farming, for example. I assume that the gesture of demarcating a field is an ancient one, perhaps the most important gesture for creating space in ancient times. Among others, Rousseau noticed this when he claimed that building a fence around a terrain was the origin of bourgeois society. Carl Schmitt developed these intuitions in his discussion of the *nomos* of the earth, whereby he insisted on the etymological observation that the Greek *nomos*, or law, contains a trilogy of meanings: take, divide and order. Boundary stones are not random objects. In them dwells something of the energy of a primary creation of space, which is brought to bear in the early occupation of land or space by civilised beings. As long as people live in cultures of hunters and gatherers, such gestures are not well defined. As soon as they settle, however, the gestures by means of which space is occupied, subdivided and ordered begin to explode. Seen from that perspective, architecture is always also a by-product of ancient negotiations of the political order, which always have a degree of ritual to them. That is reflected in the fact that, to this day, not only the start of a construction project is marked by a ritual — the cornerstone ceremony — but also the conclusion of a building project, in the form of a topping-out ceremony. As soon as the highest point of the building is constructed, a consecration of the space is required. And even in times of a general secularisation, many developers retain this tradition. ▸

LF: I would like to discuss the semantic value of spaces beyond their measured boundaries. I see books by Paul Valéry lying on your desk. In his dialogic essay "Eupalinos, ou L'architecte" (translated as "Eupalinos, or The Architect"), he brings together the figures of Socrates and Phaedrus in a dialogue of the dead in order to discuss the principles of artistic creativity and thought, using the example of architecture. Transported beyond the bounds of the realm of the shades for a moment by his memories, Phaedrus enthusiastically recalls the skills and knowledge of the architect Eupalinos, whom he knew when alive and who managed to create works of architecture that spoke to people and moved them. If it is indeed possible to perceive such allegedly sweeping addresses by architecture and to examine a building for its hidden statements made in the language of architecture, I ask myself what claim, in your opinion, does contemporary architecture lay on communication?

PS: This much seems certain to me: it says something different today than it did at the beginning of heroic modernism. I recently saw the Frank Lloyd Wright exhibition at the Guggenheim Museum in New York, and I was very touched by the masterly rhetoric of the building that Wright developed. He quite clearly associated with his buildings a kind of message of cultural imperialism. I was particularly astonished by his project for a skyscraper in Illinois, the Mile-High Tower. It proves that even the boldest developers in the United Arab Emirates today are lagging way behind these visions. Seen as a whole, contemporary architecture has developed several different rhetorics of the building, all of which take a position against the imperial gesture of early modernism. The classic modernist buildings say to their inhabitants: We have understood you properly for the first time. Anyone who looks at Buckminster Fuller's Dymaxion house will hear it say quite clearly to its virtual resident: I understand you better than you understand yourself. I shall keep you from wasting your life energy in the future by senselessly running back and forth in your inefficiently organised home. I understand you as an energy-saving system that has to find itself. I understand you as a living, sleeping, driving and digesting monad, and – even if you don't recognise me as such – I am your best friend as a house and shell. Other speaking buildings of this type were quite blatantly conceived as bachelor machines: I am your container and accomplice. Because man is an animal that needs a container, I shall do you the service of being your ideal container. I am discreet and unfurnished and don't get on your nerves with all the knick-knacks that once seemed part of dwelling. I respect you as a modern man by offering you the complete secularisation of the home and living space – a living space that surrounds you like a white cube. In me, you automatically become an artist because everything inside me becomes an installation. In short, these are all potential messages that the early modernist building may have addressed to its occupant. Buildings have since learned new messages. Werner Sobel, with whom I've been conversing for some time, taught his residential buildings a few important new propositions, which we may assume will enter the architectural idiom in general in the coming decades. For example, his R128 model says: I am appealing to your ecological intelligence. If you look at me correctly, you will understand: I am not simply a container but also a watch. I keep your life rhythms in mind. I am your partner in the temporal aspects of your existence; I interpret your circadian rhythm; I react to the difference between day and night. I appeal to your intelligence as an ecologically aware, cosmopolitan contemporary by offering you a completely uncluttered life. That is, famously, the pathos of a Sobek house: everything non-essential is tossed out of it. ◄

ARCHITECTURE IS ALWAYS ALSO A BY-PRODUCT OF ANCIENT NEGOTIATIONS OF THE POLITICAL ORDER

Continuation on page 82.

HEINRICH BÖLL FOUNDATION
E2A ECKERT ECKERT ARCHITEKTEN (PIET ECKERT, WIM ECKERT)

01 The water for cooling comes from an adiabatic recooler situated in the basement. This has cooling fins, on which normal tap water is sprayed.

02 Embedded on the first floor is the convention and conference centre, which cantilevers into urban space.

ENGINEER
HVAC/S: Basler & Hofmann,
Ingenieure und Planer AG, Zurich

CLIENT
Heinrich-Böll-Stiftung e.V.,
Berlin, Germany

PROJECT LOCATION
Berlin, Germany

COMPLETION DATE
2008

01

ASSIGNMENT

The client, the Heinrich Böll Foundation, is a non-profit organisation closely linked to the Green Party aimed at promoting democracy, civil society, equality and a healthy environment internationally. The architects were asked to design a new convention and conference centre providing space for 300 individuals as well as office spaces for the foundation's 185 employees. The brief was to design a landmark building to enhance visibility for the foundation and to provide an emblematic design that reflects the values for which the foundation stands. Top priority for the client was also to meet the highest ecological building standards and to create an extremely cost-efficient design. ◣

LOCATION

The site is located in a city park close to the government buildings in the centre of Berlin. In order to impinge on the park area as little as possible, the new building occupies a minimal footprint with the highest possible surface. ◣

CONCEPT

To meet the tight budget and minimise the building's footprint, the offices were stacked on top of one another and efficiently organised. Embedded on the first floor is the convention and conference centre, which cantilevers into urban space. From within, the cantilevered floor offers a deep perspective into the park, conveying the strong presence of trees and vegetation to visitors and users. In addition, this floor's setting represents a striving for transparency in the processes of democratic decision-making, socio-political engagement, and international understanding. "In terms of spending and saving on fittings, furnishing and materials, the architectural concept became an economic concept," say the architects. "Everything we could save in the office spaces we could spend on the first floor and vice versa." The concept is one of polarity: the convention centre level with its precious fittings and applied materials contrasts with the office space, which are treated as workshops, with plain concrete surfaces and visible technical installations, allowing a high level of flexibility for their users. An efficient and effective energy concept for the building involved implementing little, but highly innovative, technology. It also meant exploiting the laws of thermodynamics instead of installing a large amount of technical equipment, using intelligent systems with as little equipment as possible, an efficient building insulation and triple insulation glass. The energy concept developed for this building depends on users taking responsibility for determining the inner climate through their own interaction. ◣

REALISATION

The realisation of the building was the result of close collaboration between client, architect and contractor. Intense monitoring, especially in terms of meeting ecological standards, not only took into account the daily energy consumption of the building, but also the energy used to produce the applied materials, technical systems and equipment. The close co-operation between the various parties also ensured that innovative solutions were successfully implemented within a tight budget and the client's requirements could be met. ◣

ENERGY CONCEPT

In conventional office buildings, the air conditioning has to run at full capacity throughout the summer, guzzling energy, to prevent the building from overheating. At the Heinrich Böll Foundation, water is used directly for cooling, not air conditioning machinery. Outlet slits run at sill level along the glazing in every office. The sill casing houses high-performance heat exchangers, through which water at a temperature of 20 degrees Celsius circulates in summer. A small ventilator inside ensures that cooled air is distributed throughout the room. Even when the temperature outside is over 30 degrees Celsius, the room temperature does not rise above 25 degrees Celsius. The water for cooling comes from an adiabatic recooler situated in the basement. This has cooling fins, on which normal tap water is sprayed. The energy used when it evaporates is drawn out of the fins, reducing the temperature of the coolant water inside to 20 degrees Celsius. The cooled water is then ready to circulate through the under-sill heat exchangers once more. The system used in the Heinrich Böll Foundation does not involve a jump in temperature. As a result, it cools ten times more efficiently than a conventional system would. The building's atrium functions as a lung, using natural ventilation to maintain a pleasant working environment. In summer, the internal courtyard is aired naturally through the open roof of the atrium. In winter, when the roof is closed, a ventilation system coupled with heat exchangers maintains a flow of fresh air into the atrium. This extracts heat from the exhaust air and uses it to warm the fresh air being brought in. The office spaces and internal corridors can open up into the atrium, creating a cross current to provide the interiors with fresh air as needed. Thanks to the atrium, this occurs without the heat loss that would otherwise be experienced in winter. Winter heating is controlled by the computer network servers making effective use of heat that is normally wasted. The under-sill installation that cools the offices in summer also heats them in winter – and it does so with the same level of efficiency. Whereas conventional heating systems need hot water at temperatures of up to 50 degrees Celsius, the under-sill installation functions with a flow temperature of 28 degrees Celsius. It also makes effective use of the heat produced by the computer network servers. The servers of the Heinrich Böll Foundation are kept in cool racks, which remove heat rather like a fridge does. This arrangement integrates the servers with the building services system and makes their heat directly available to it. Water flows into the cool racks at a temperature of 23 degrees Celsius, where it is warmed by the servers to around 27 degrees Celsius. It is then fed into the heating system and circulated through the offices to keep them comfortably warm in winter. The only cost of this heat is the energy needed by the pumps to circulate the water – 90 per cent can be used directly as heat energy. In summer, the servers are cooled by the adiabatic recooler. There is also a photovoltaic system on the roof designed in partnership with Grammer Solar that has an annual energy yield of some 53,000 kilowatt hours and feeds into the district heating system. ◣

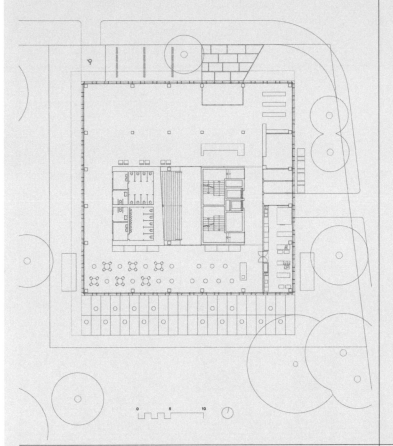

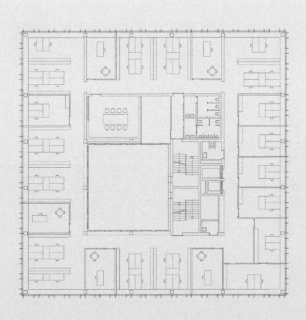

03 Second floor plan

04 Third floor plan

01 The building's atrium functions as a lung, using natural ventilation to maintain a pleasant working environment.

02 From within, the cantilevered floor offers a deep perspective into the park.

03 View of the office spaces.

04 Plan concrete surfaces and visible technical installations allow a high level of flexibility for the building's users.

02

03

04

01 The new landmark building of the Swiss
Federal Institute of Technology in Zurich.

02 Close up of the building's
travertine façades.

ETH E-SCIENCE LAB, HIT NEW BUILDING
BAUMSCHLAGER EBERLE ARCHITECTS

BUILDING TECHNOLOGY
HL Technik AG Klaus
Daniels, Lauber IWISA AG

CLIENT
ETH Immobilien

PROJECT LOCATION
Zurich, Switzerland

COMPLETION DATE
2008

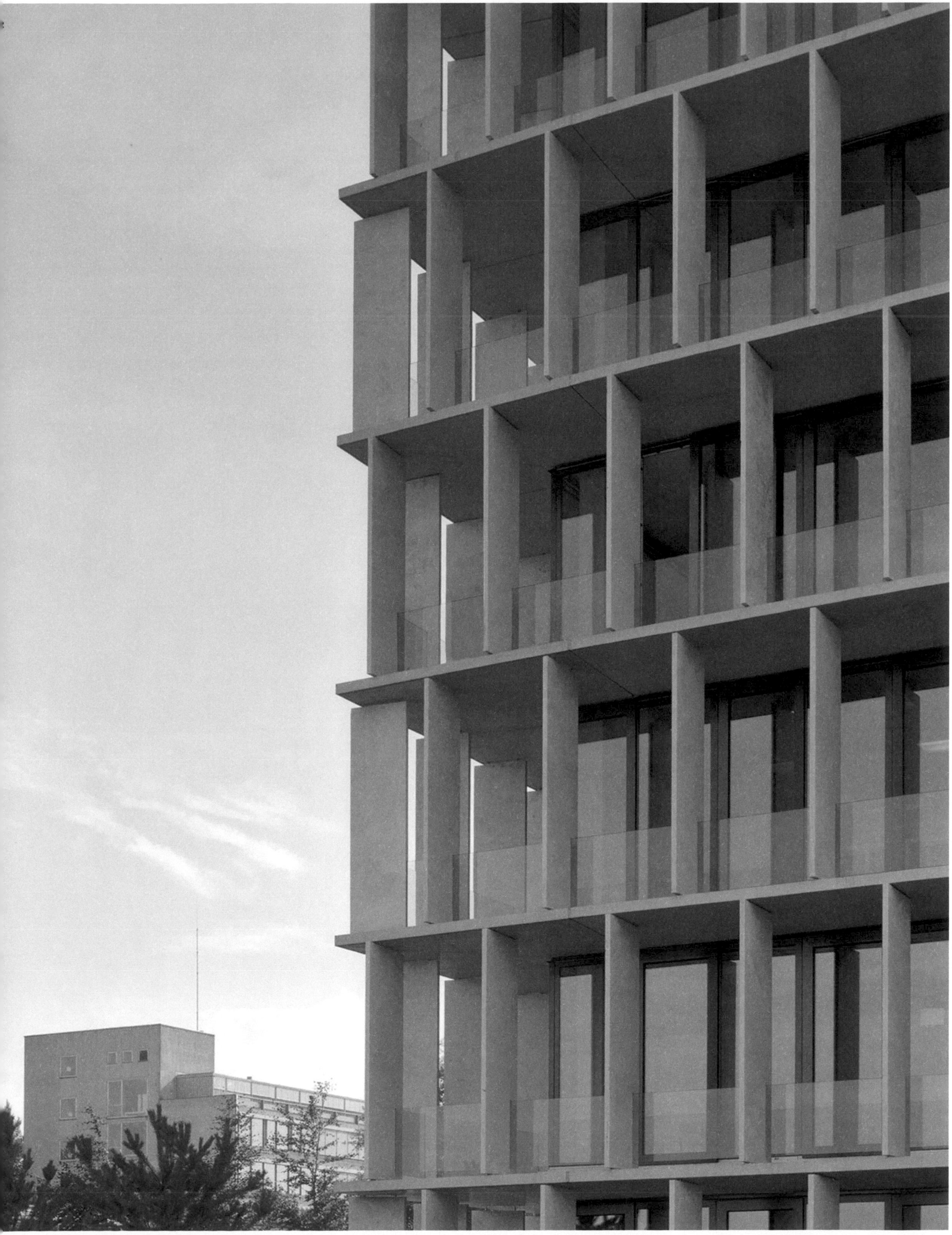

01

02

01 Cross section of the building.

02 Seminar rooms that encourage communication and concentration have been integrated into the inner volume.

03 The colourful boxes offer an intersecting synthesis of open, yet condensed spaces.

03

ASSIGNMENT

The ETH e-Science Lab is the first stage of the extension of the Swiss Federal Institute of Technology (ETH) in the Hönggerberg district of Zurich. The client wanted a landmark building within the new "science city" – a district where science and society will meet. Baumschlager Eberle was asked to concentrate on finding the right urbanistic shape for this campus area. Another highly critical factor was to create a building with significantly reduced energy consumption. ◣

LOCATION

The site of the new campus district is located on a hillside in the outskirts of the city of Zurich in Switzerland. Baumschlager Eberle's intention was to balance the specific features of the site with optimum flexibility in the structure of the building. ◣

CONCEPT

Defining the site and shaping the future of scientific work – these were the key challenges at the Hönggerberg. The architects wanted to create architecture which serves as an aesthetic, yet comfortable, frame for both study and research. ◣

REALISATION

The occupants have installed a great deal of electronic equipment in the e-Science Lab, but the outcome is not a high-tech building symbolising the data highway. On the contrary, the architects have devised a no-frills rectangular block which integrates a multitude of planning tasks. Taking due account of the hillside location of the ETH campus, the spatial geometry of the structure sends out a clear signal which appears perfectly natural in its timelessness. This compact geometry is the envelope for a central courtyard with rectangular access to the research offices. Six seminar rooms have been integrated into this inner volume. There is an interesting synthesis of open, yet condensed, spaces which encourage communication and concentration in the building's users. The chromatic works of Zurich-based artist Adrian Schiess occupy the walls here. The colourful educational boxes and the multimedia teaching facility can be regarded as orthogonal areas which extend their own ambiguous three-dimensionality and thereby question established ways of seeing things.

The rectangular block format reinforces a type of architecture which breaks free from the usual tyranny of technical services. Here the architecture defines the deployment of the utilities instead: the compact form reduces energy consumption. The travertine façades are durable devices for shading, and open ceilings improve retention capacity. The neutral-use floors provide the necessary flexibility for a variety of utility adaptations since forward-looking technical services support the best use of the building. As a result, the architects and engineers achieve an integral solution for an energy consumption of 94 kilowatt hours per square metre, which is lower than the Swiss Minergie standard. As the built structure always outlasts a building's technical services, it is the architecture that fulfils the task of creating sustainability. ◣

04 Established ways of seeing things are questioned throughout the building.

05 Wall elements connect directly to the façade at 1.2-metre intervals.

ENERGY CONCEPT

The architects did not want to design a test or prototype building for energy reduction. They believed that comfort and energy reduction should be partners in an integral solution. The rectangular nature of the structure demonstrates its value in the research offices and makes a major contribution to the flexibility of the building. The wall elements connect directly to the façade at 1.2-metre intervals. They constitute the smallest spatial units, each with its own microclimate provided by displacement ventilation induction units. Every user can adapt the climate to meet his or her own personal comfort level. The key factor here is that the architecture itself fixes the parameters of energy consumption. The compact form, open ceilings and the shade-giving façades are long-term and long-lasting basics for energy reduction. The concrete used as the main building material is locally sourced, which also helps to diminish grey energy input. ◣

HARMONIA // 57

TRIPTYQUE - GREG BOUSQUET, CAROLINA BUENO, GUILLAUME SIBAUD AND OLIVIER RAFFAELLI / PROJECT CHIEF - TIAGO GUIMARÃES

ENGINEER
Hydraulic – ER Engineering, Eng. Guilherme Castagna (Design Ecológico) / Irrigation – Hidrosistemas, Eng. Guilherme Coelho Silva / Landscaping – Peter Webb Structures – Eng. Rioske Kanno / Hydraulic execution – TKC / Contractor – Aparecido Flausino Dias

CLIENT
Private

PROJECT LOCATION
São Paulo / São Paulo / Brazil

COMPLETION DATE
2008

01

01 The terraces are spread on each floor, creating a visual game between volumes, lighting and transparency in the internal spaces.

02 The pipelines that serve the whole building are visible in the exterior walls.

01 The terraces are spread on each floor, creating a visual game between volumes, lighting and transparency in the internal spaces.

02 The pipelines that serve the whole building are visible in the exterior walls.

01

ASSIGNMENT

French-Brazilian architects Triptyque were asked to
create an innovative hybrid space to house a small
company. It had to be versatile and allow spontaneous
changes in layout and use. ◣

LOCATION

The building is located in a neighbourhood on the west
side of São Paulo, where artistic life and creativity
increasingly shape the streetscape. Geographically
speaking, the site is distinguished by the climate of
a tropical country with
massive rain showers and
very high temperatures,
as well as rich soil with
natural underground sys-
tems. ◣

CONCEPT

In Brazil, 1.3 thousand
square metres of rain fall
per year: 234,000 litres
of clean water that are
wasted annually. Against
this backdrop, Triptyque
developed their original
idea for the building,
which is based on local
water systems. Like a
living body, the building
breathes, perspires and
modifies itself. Rain and
soil water are drained,
treated and reused, form-
ing a complex ecosystem.
The building's insides are
exposed through the façades
while the interior spaces
are well finished with clear
and luminous surfaces, as
if the construction were
inside out. The pipelines
that serve the whole building – as well as the pumps
and the water treatment
system – are visible in
the exterior walls, which
embrace them like veins
and arteries. ◣

REALISATION

Harmonia//57 is an office building with a planted
façade irrigated by a mist system. The walls are
thick and covered externally by a layer of vegetation that works like the skin of the structure.
This dense wall is made of an organic concrete
that has pores, where several plant species
grow, giving the façades a unique look. Two grand
vegetal blocks are connected by a metallic foot-
bridge, cut by concrete and glass windows and
terraces. Between the blocks, an internal plaza
opens like a clearing and acts as a meeting
place. The terraces are spread in each floor,
creating a visual game between volumes, lighting
and transparency in the internal spaces. The
frontal block is completely suspended, levitating
over pilotis, while the back block is solid and
complemented by a birdhouse-like volume positioned on top of it.Questioning the construction
as a finished and manufactured object, the building also brings to light different phases of
its evolution. In the spirit of the client, who
organises fairs to showcase local artistic tal-
ents, the building was also used as an event
space during the construction period. The construction was halted for about ten days, and the
site became an open gallery, where the site workers and artists collaborated to
create an exhibition with accompanying public lectures and debates. ◣

ENERGY CONCEPT

Through the use of a vegetal concrete that absorbs water
and allows plants to grow inside its niches, the temperature and noise inside the building are controlled,
reducing the need for air conditioning. Insulation and
wind influence the basic choice of species used in the
external walls. Some species create shade while others
crawl over the surface of the building providing a bank
of humidity available for bordering plants. The project
foregrounds the hydro system, which creates a dynamic
relation throughout its length with the low-tech elements
(tubes/pluming/tanks/broadcasters, etc.) offering
var-ious border elements – some of which constitute
the guardrails of the building. In order to seize the
building's rain water, the architects united low-tech
materials, such as vegetal concrete, with a simple
irrigation system and innovative water treatment. To
store the large volume of water without generating
a high-cost infrastructure, a
broader rain-water re-use programme was developed. A green
roof directs a portion of the
run-off into the groundwater,
generates fresh air and provides good thermal conditions
inside the building, reducing
the need for air conditioning
and withholding a fair share
of the rain water. The surplus
of water from the roofs is
directed for storage in three
shells located on the ground.
These prevent water from running off to the street even
in periods of intense rainfall.
At the end of a separate reservoir, water continues to a larger
reservoir, which is periodically
served by a system of ozone,
and then pumped into higher
containers, which continue
to supply the toilets and provide irrigation. The infiltration
of water in seedbeds on flat
ground is directed by a slow
infiltration to the subsoil. This
helps maintain higher levels of
groundwater. ◣

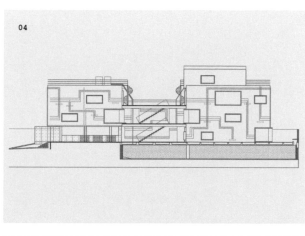

01 Various stairways connect the different floors.

02 Like a living body, the building breathes, perspires and modifies itself.

03 Between the blocks, an internal plaza opens like a clearing and acts as a meeting place.

04 Longitudinal elevation

05 Longitudinal section.

06 Front and back elevation.

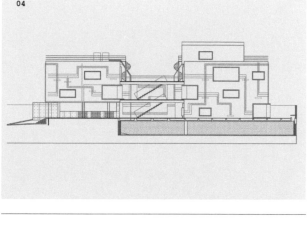

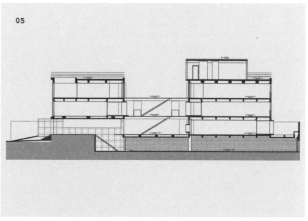

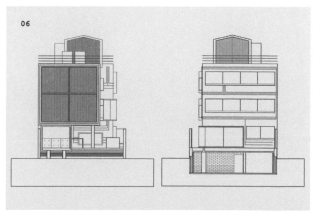

01 The frontal block is completely sus-pended, levitating over pilotis.

02 The building within the urban context.

03 Illustration of the building's water system.

39

CHAPTER 01

C A N   I   G E T   A   W I T N E S S

03

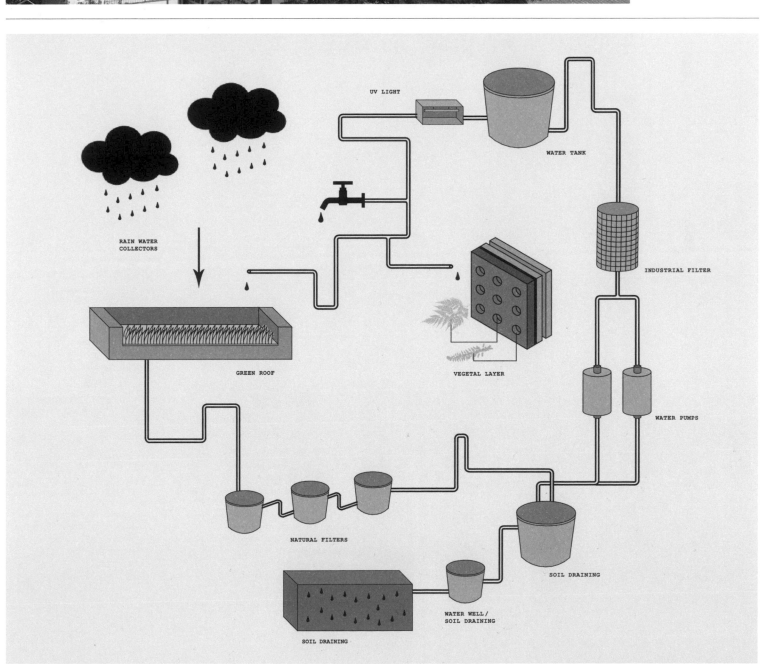

01/ Eden Bio Features
02 terraced houses ranged
along pedestrian alleys.

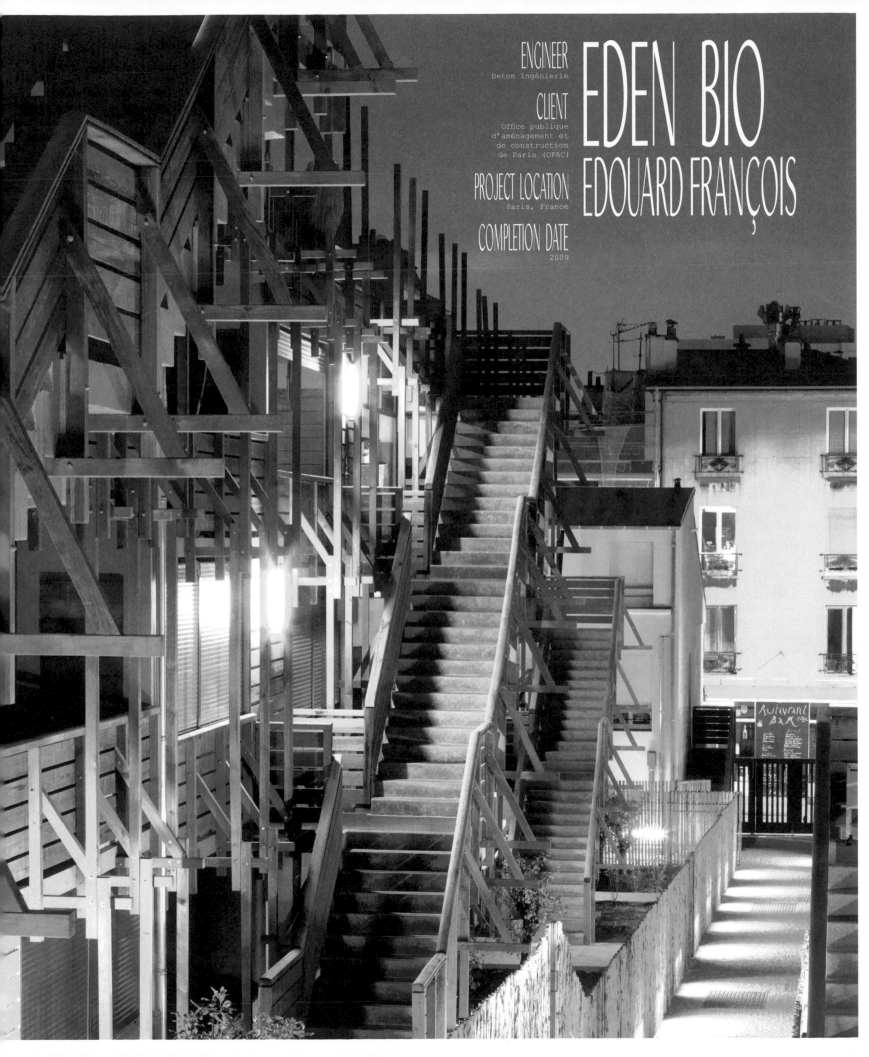

ENGINEER
Betom Ingénierie

CLIENT
Office publique
d'aménagement et
de construction
de Paris (OPAC)

PROJECT LOCATION
Paris, France

COMPLETION DATE
2009

EDEN BIO
EDOUARD FRANÇOIS

01 The upper levels are reached by external timber gantries and staircases.

02 Elevation of Eden Bio's varying façades.

03 Along the original alleys, maisonettes and buildings with landscaped façades face each other.

04 Every house has its own façade, its own cladding to differentiate it from the others.

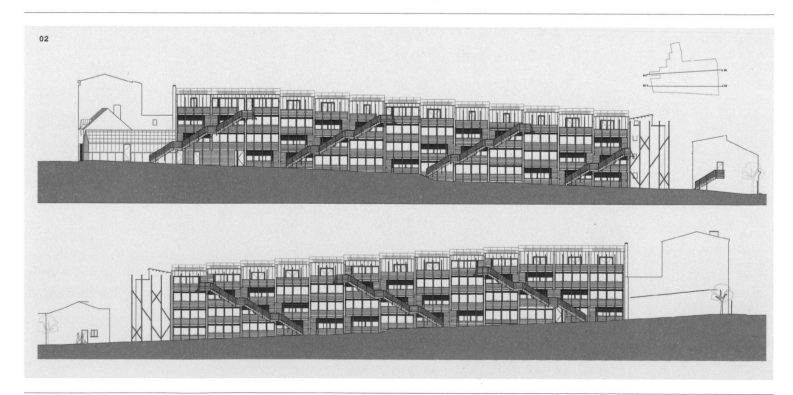

03

04

ASSIGNMENT

The project involved the design and construction of a social housing development in Paris. The programme consists of one hundred social housing units, a car park, ateliers for artists, and community spaces. ▲

CONCEPT

Eden Bio features terraced houses ranged along pedestrian alleys heavily landscaped with trees and plants. The upper levels are reached by external timber gantries and staircases surrounded by greenery. The urbanistic approach leaves the street front in its original small scale and grows denser towards the centre, along the original alleys, where maisonettes and buildings with landscaped façades face each other. A clear entrance to the building complex is deliberately avoided by imposing a labyrinthine structure on the building ensemble. ▲

LOCATION

The block of houses is situated in the low-income suburbs around Paris. The site is located in an area of fragmented buildings of low height. ▲

REALISATION

The central building is wrapped with greenery and timber garden stakes. Along its length, its height is graded in order to better embrace the sloping topography. Each apartment has windows on both sides and a balcony oriented south. The landscaped façade is planted in the ground. Thousands of wisteria will climb numerous vertically-assembled stakes. Situated every two metres between stairs and balconies, this scaffolding of timber will be gently colonised by plants. The ensemble, once completed, will have a great variety of forms and materials, which will vary with the seasons. The ensemble embracing the central building is held together by a ribbon of red shingles that wraps around it. ▲

ENERGY CONCEPT

Like all of Edouard François' projects, Eden Bio connects people in an urban condition to natural processes such as seasons, growth and decay. What distinguishes this project from the masterly implementation of green façades within an urban context is also the overall exchange of the polluted ground soil with cost-intensive bio-certified earth in deep layers to accelerate the natural growth of the plants. In order to create a somewhat self-maintained urban wilderness, plants and fruits were selected based on their capacity to thrive without fertiliser or pesticides and to preserve their characteristics in the new landscape. The resulting landscape will be unpredictable, made of those wild species that spontaneously survive. In combined efforts with nursery expert Arnaud Delbard, the architect created a unique apple tree for this wild garden. Overall, Eden Bio is a project to discover, in a few years, after its maturation, like a good wine. ▲

GREEN PIX - ZERO ENERGY MEDIA WALL
SIMONE GIOSTRA AND PARTNERS

ENGINEER
Arup

CLIENT
Jingya Corporation

PROJECT LOCATION
Beijing, China

COMPLETION DATE
2008

01 One of the largest colour LED displays worldwide and the first photovoltaic system integrated into a glass curtain wall in China.

02 Elevation of the media façade.

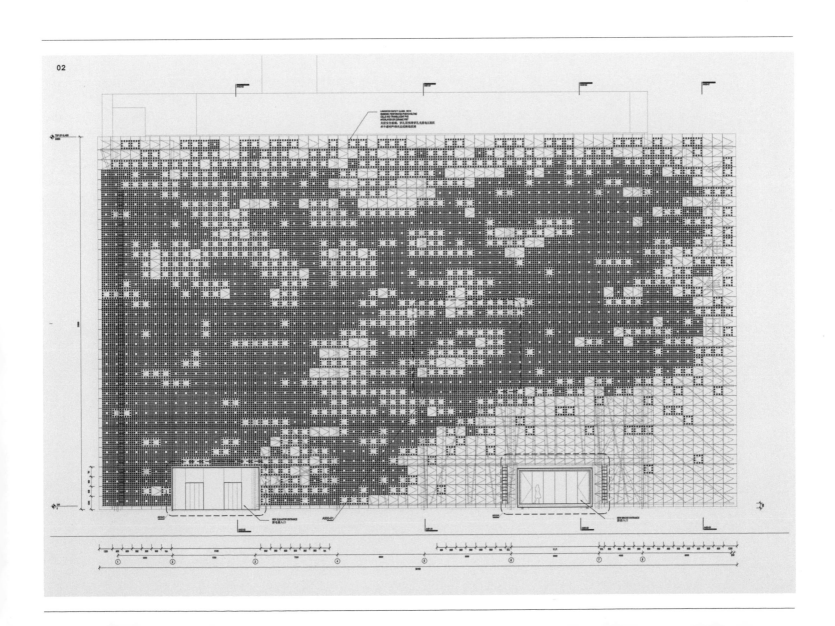

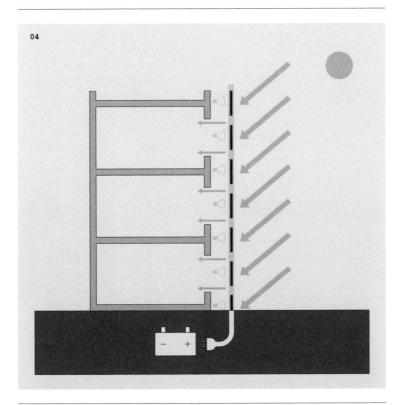

03

03.01
03.02
03.03
03.04

03.05

03.06

03.07

03.08

03.01 Catwalk for maintenance staff
03.02 Structural embeds anchor onto existing columns
03.03 150 mm x 150 mm truss
03.04 Vertical bracing
03.05 890 mm x 890 mm glass panel
03.06 Fluorescent lighting spaced 900 mm x 900 mm
03.07 Spider clamp
03.08 Photovoltaic cell

04

01 GreenPix offers a dynamic and interactive experience for the viewer.

02 Entrance situation. The entertainment complex houses a movie theatre and a high-end restaurant.

03 Photovoltaic cells are laminated within the glass of the curtain wall.

04 The media wall relies on solar energy accumulated during the day.

ASSIGNMENT

In 2005 New York-based architects Simone Giostra and Partners were charged with enlivening the box-like structure of an entertainment complex in Beijing, China, and connecting it to its surrounding environment. ◤

LOCATION

The Xicui Entertainment Complex is located in the western part of Beijing near the site for baseball and basketball games during the 2008 Olympics; it houses a movie theatre and high-end restaurant. The building opened to the public in the summer of 2008. ◤

CONCEPT

GreenPix is based on the original idea that a truly organic system should depend on its own ability to gather resources and, at the same time, remain vulnerable to changing environmental conditions. Similarly, the media wall relies on solar energy accumulated during the day, and its lighting performance is affected by the daily amount of sunlight reaching the building. The project attempts to address the need for interaction and change in the built environment. Simone Giostra and Partners therefore developed custom software showing content on the building façade, offering a dynamic and interactive experience to the viewer and a communication surface devoted to unprecedented forms of artistic expression. The design concept also grew out of the need to project information to varying distances and engaging a vast audience within the city of Beijing. ◤

REALISATION

Featuring one of the largest colour LED displays worldwide and the first photovoltaic system integrated into a glass curtain wall in China, GreenPix transforms the building envelope into a self-sufficient organic system, harvesting solar energy by day and using it to illuminate the screen after dark, mirroring a day's climatic cycle. Through the use of LED lighting, the façade has the ability to show playback videos, live content, including live performances, and user-generated content. The wall showcases low-resolution imagery, both to conserve energy and to provide an art-specific communication form in contrast to commercial applications of high-resolution screens in conventional media façades. ◤

ENERGY CONCEPT

GreenPix performs like an organic system, similar to a tree or a flower, first absorbing solar energy and then generating light from the same power that evening, without supplementary power. With the support of leading German manufacturers Schueco and SunWays, the architects developed a new technology for laminating photovoltaic cells in a glass curtain wall and oversaw the production of the first glass solar panels by Chinese manufacturer SunTech. The polycrystalline photovoltaic cells are slices of silicon laminated within the glass of the curtain wall. In GreenPix the cells are placed with changing density on the entire building's skin, perhaps the most extensive use of this technology in a building curtain wall to date. The density pattern increases building performance, allowing natural light when required by an interior programme, while reducing heat gain and transforming excessive solar radiation into energy for the media wall. ◤

ENGINEER

AHW Engineers GmbH (structural engineering), Graner und Partner Ingenieure GmbH (building physics), Fenster Keller GmbH+Co, Fenster + Fassaden KG (façades), Bilfinger Berger AG (general contractor)

CLIENT

GGH Gesellschaft für Grund- und Hausbesitz mbH

PROJECT LOCATION

Heidelberg, Germany

COMPLETION DATE

2007

NEW FIRE STATION
PETER KULKA ARCHITEKTUR
PETER KULKA, HENRYK URBANIETZ

01 The hose and training tower rise 35 metres.

02 The administrative rooms on the eastern side are set upon delicate V-shaped pillars.

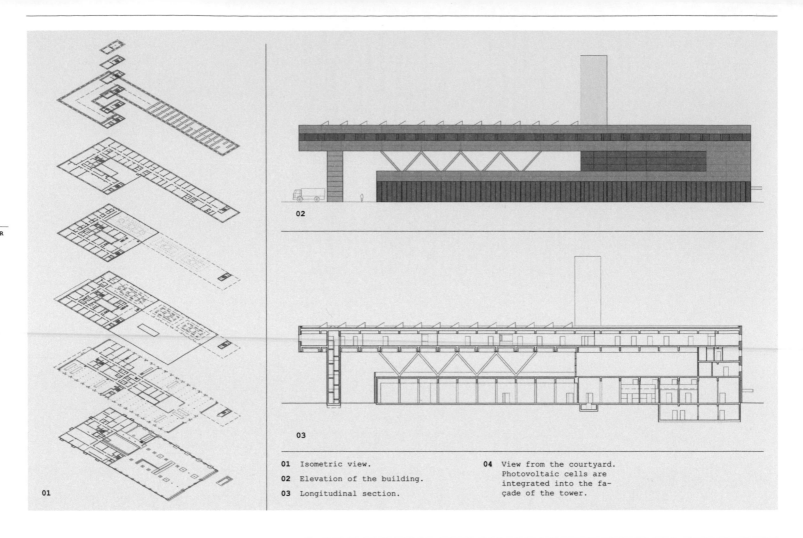

01 Isometric view.

02 Elevation of the building.

03 Longitudinal section.

04 View from the courtyard. Photovoltaic cells are integrated into the façade of the tower.

ASSIGNMENT

The architects were commissioned to build a new fire station for the city of Heidelberg. ◣

CONCEPT

Through the combination of aesthetically and functionally sophisticated architecture, and by applying the energy standard of a passive house, Peter Kulka strives to open entirely new opportunities in the field of fire stations and create a sculptural structure as a distinct figure located at the city's entrance. ◣

LOCATION

The New Fire Station is situated at the transition between the periphery and inner city of Heidelberg, in southern Germany. ◣

REALISATION

Wrapped around a maintenance core on three sides is the garage, where the fire engines are parked behind see-through foldable gates. Together with the entry hall, this constitutes the base of the building, beneath the upper levels, which are constructed according to the passive-house standard. On the eastern side, the top floor continues as a bar that houses the administrative rooms on delicate V-shaped pillars. The 35-metre-high hose and training tower place emphasis on the vertical. ◣

ENERGY CONCEPT

By following the Heidelberg City "Guide for Healthy and Environmentally Sound Building Materials" and applying diverse resource-friendly measures such as insulation, energy-efficient window glazing, earth heat exchange, heat recovery and on-site rainwater absorption, the architects have created a landmark example of sustainable architecture. The whole structure is a steel and concrete frame construction that is thermally decoupled. Of particular importance was the planning of the façade, which consists of non-bearing aluminium panels, which make up the skin of the building together with lines of windows that increase the sculptural effect of the structure. Photovoltaic cells were integrated into the façade of the tower following the same aesthetic specifications. In the process, 135 monocrystalline solar modules were installed into an aluminium post-and-beam construction. The 350-square-metre system blends into the whole as an independent element. Another solar power plant was included in the planning for the office wing. Energy-saving and resource-friendly performance makes the Heidelberg fire station an economically highly efficient building. Compared to a conventional fire station, for instance, 90 per cent of the energy for space heating is saved, and the integrated photovoltaic modules feed as much electricity into the municipal grid as 14 three-person households use annually. By orientating the fire station to ensure that the solar-active components are not obscured by shade, the passive solar heat gain was optimised and became an essential heat source. The compactness of the building makes the passive-house standard possible even without a primarily southern exposure. ◣

OSLO INTERNATIONAL SCHOOL

JARMUEND/VIGSNAES ARCHITECTS

ENGINEER
AS Frederiksen

CLIENT
Oslo International School

PROJECT LOCATION
Bekkestua, Norway

COMPLETION DATE
Ongoing since 2007

01 View of the entrance situation. Organic forms soften the dense spatial relationships between new and old areas.

01 The highly insulated walls are clad with specially milled wooden panelling.

02 Children playing in the school's courtyard.

03 Daylight fills the rooms from narrow slits from floor to ceiling combined with circular roof lights.

04 Interior view.

05 Elevation of the building.

06 Floorplan illustrating the various building phases.

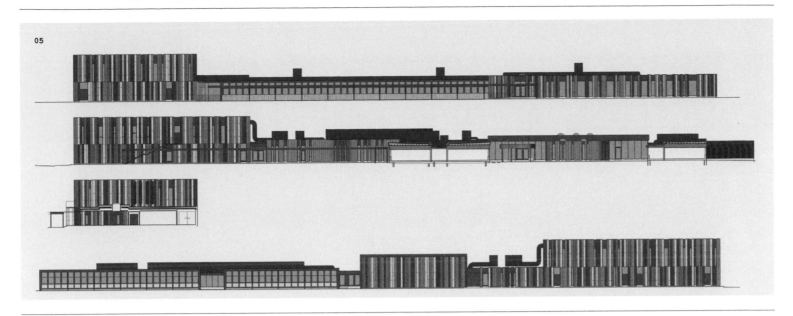

05

ASSIGNMENT

Oslo International-al School is a private school with about 500 children from more than 50 different nations, divided into a kindergarten, a reception, and a primary and secondary school. The school is based on a traditional use of classrooms combined with special facilities for advanced studies. ◣

LOCATION

The school is located in a town in the municipality of Bærum, Norway, in the Oslo area. The previous facilities of the Oslo International School were far from adequate to support the changing learning environment and student body. While some renovations and a new wing were added in the 1990s, most areas had not been updated for years. Consequently, parts of the 3600-square-metre main building, built in the 1960s, were in need of renewal. In addition, the school was required to remove the 1150 square metres of temporary accommodations that were housing various teaching programmes. ◣

CONCEPT

The primary goal of the building project is to upgrade existing areas, replace temporary structures and establish new educational areas for specific needs. The existing structure from the 1960s was degraded but had obvious architectonic qualities, such as organisation on one level providing an ease of orientation, good natural lighting and close contact to the outdoors. The need for space and revitalisation was, however, critical to the project and fostered the development of a modular structure, flexible to programmatic changes. The new structure gently transforms the organisation within a limited budget and tries to keep inherent qualities. ◣

ENERGY CONCEPT

With reference to the qualities of the old structure, the new buildings are organised around three new atriums suited for play and recreation for the different groups of children. The existing atrium is established as the quiet garden with white gravel, benches and greenery perfect for quiet play and conversation. Two large existing oaks are preserved. The organically shaped walls are highly insulated and clad with specially milled wooden panelling. The architecture is developed as a new vocabulary of soft and organic forms, softening dense spatial relationships between new and old areas. At the same time, these new areas contain special programmes framed by the rectilinear structure of the old. Daylight fills the rooms from narrow slits from floor to ceiling combined with circular roof lights. ◣

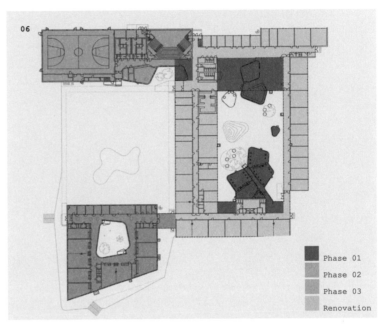

06

Phase 01
Phase 02
Phase 03
Renovation

REALISATION

The project is divided into three phases to enable continuous use of the school during the construction period. The first phase is established as pavilions within an existing atrium. They include science laboratories, a library and a main square. The main entrance is moved to the west side of the building. The second phase is a separate pavilion for the youngest children. It houses ten classrooms in addition to offices. The common areas get daylight from the atrium. The sizes of rooms are flexible and can be changed according to the number of children on each level. Phase one and phase two have now been completed. The staff and children have moved into the new primary building and are enjoying their new environment. The projection on phase three has now started, which will include the renovation and extension of the existing gym into an auditorium, drama and music rooms and larger gym facilities. This next phase of the building project is likely to commence towards the end of 2009/early 2010. ◣

MEYDAN RETAIL COMPLEX
FOREIGN OFFICE ARCHITECTS (FOA)
LED BY FARSHID MOUSSAVI AND ALEJANDRO ZAERA-POLO

ENGINEER	CLIENT	PROJECT LOCATION	COMPLETION DATE
Adams Kara Taylor	Metro Group Asset Management	Ümraniye, Istanbul, Turkey	2007

01 View of the roof gardens

01 Interior view from shopping mall. Skylights are even introduced to retail areas, creating a visual contact between the retail spaces and the
gardens on the roofs.

02 View of the open plaza.

ASSIGNMENT

The Meydan Retail Complex was commissioned for an area on the outskirts of Istanbul in Turkey. It is a large-scale shopping centre built in anticipation of planned future residential developments. As such, the centre needs to perform not only as an efficient retail complex but as an urban centre in one of the fastest growing areas of Istanbul. For the client, Metro Asset Management, a particular concern was making the Meydan Retail Complex and multiplex a model of green policy implemented in a large-scale shopping centre. ◣

LOCATION

Located in a suburban area in the Asian sector of Istanbul, the site of the Meydan Complex borders an IKEA store, as well as residential plots to be developed in the near future. Through its geometry and circulation strategy, the complex anticipates its subsequent integration into a dense inner city context as an alternative to the usual out-of-town retail box development. ◣

REALISATION

The different retail spaces are clustered together and parking is placed underground, liberating the ground entirely for a large urban square in the centre of the scheme. The central square is activated though a number of new pedestrian routes, linking the underground car park to the ground level and accessible from the wider city context though two new routes across the roofs of the retail spaces. To organise the retail volumes as an extension of the surrounding topography rather than as sheds deployed onto an asphalt platform, common to out-of-town retail developments, all roofs are connected to the surrounding topography at several points and designed as gardens with extensive vegetation. In addition to physical continuities between the new development and the surrounding context, skylights are introduced to retail areas, creating visual contact to the gardens on the roofs. The experience of shopping at Meydan Retail Complex is in this way continuously connected with the urban space beyond. ◣

ENERGY CONCEPT

Using natural roof meadows and a flowing transition from buildings to a spacious plaza, FOA has created a new square for Ümraniye and a very interesting sustainable development prototype for Turkey and elsewhere. The Meydan is the first shopping centre that the Metro Group has built without a single central heating boiler. Instead, the centre uses the huge Istanbul Ümraniye district geothermal system to heat and cool the 70,000-square-metre complex. It saves 1.3 million kilowatt hours of primary energy a year. Geothermal energy is safe, available at any time, and does not produce any environmentally harmful emissions.

The calculated CO_2 savings for the system is 350 tonnes a year. The system works like a gigantic heat reservoir: in summer it stores the exhaust heat from the ventilation system so that it can be used for heating in winter. On average the shopping square needs conspicuously more cooling output than heating output annually. This is why the engineers also installed two cooling towers with a total capacity of 2500 kilowatts. If required, they will ensure that the approximately 50 shops in the shopping square also have a pleasant ambient climate even at high midsummer temperatures. The economic side of the project is also noteworthy: the system is calculated to pay for itself in three to five years, depending on the development of energy costs. Because the geothermal system replaces the air conditioning units that are normally found on roofs, the Meydan roof area was freed up to be used and designed for landscaping. As a result, the complex has one of the largest green roofs in a single area in the world. The entire roof of the centre - approximately 30,000 square metres - is landscaped (the only exception is the roof of the cinema complex), 1000 square metres of which are a publicly accessible park. The roof fulfils additional important functions for the building climate: it holds back rain, is self-irrigating and thus reduces the burden on the sewer system; it filters harmful dust particles and pollutants from the city air and the plants take carbon dioxide from the air and give off oxygen. Rooftop gardens also offer a noise reduction of around eight decibels, the soil acts as thermal insulation, thus reducing energy costs, and the evaporative cooling of the lawn helps improve the microclimate. Finally, the earth layer increases the useful life of the roof membrane, as the water insulation is protected better against ultraviolet rays and is more resistant to high and low temperatures. Daylight is used to maximum advantage in the complex.

Instead of being a mall, the centre is designed as an open space. This results in fewer areas that need to be air-conditioned and lit. A 6100-square-metre, double-glass façade maximises daylight and provides insulation, whilst 28 skylights for the hypermarket save on artificial lighting. There is natural ventilation to the mall, hypermarket and underground garage (through an air and light-permeable clinker façade), and the skylights also perform a natural smoke removal function, which saves on power-hungry fans. The park landscape encourages pedestrians and cyclists. ◣

CONCEPT

This new mall concept transforms the normal out-of-town retail shed into a landscaped, intelligent and sustainable development through the use of functional and architectural interventions. Box stores are traditionally big, blank masses. With this project, Foreign Office Architects (FOA) has explored how this typology of building could be more urban and contextual. Unlike the IKEA alongside it - a retail shed - the Meydan development is spread out, incorporating public space within it and above it. Whereas the usual out-of-town retail developments locate the central space inside the mall, the Meydan complex is organised as a series of separate retail volumes set around a square. This both breaks up the mass and scale of the development and effectively produces a city square in anticipation of the city to come. The geometry and placement of the scheme on the site maximise natural shading and the creation of wind shelters, using architectural massing to change and improve the local environment instead of resorting to mechanical reparative measures. Also, all roofs were designed as green roofs, providing a park in the heart of the suburb. Instead of resorting to artificial ventilation, openings on the roof bring air and sunlight into the building. Renewable energy is supplied through solar panels and a ground source heat pump. FOA worked with environmental consultants WSP in designing this project. ◣

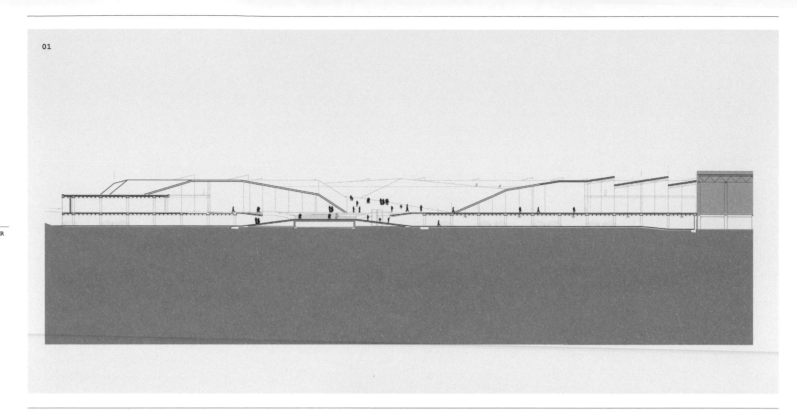

01 Longitudinal section of the building.

02 The mass and scale of the development are broken up through a series of separate retail volumes. Openings on the roof bring air and sunlight into the building.

03 Flowing transition from building to spacious plaza.

04/ Elevation of the roof. The Meydan
05 development is spread out, incorporating public space within it and above it. Through its geometry and circulation strategy, the complex anticipates its subsequent integration into a denser inner city context as an alternative to the usual out-of-town retail box development.

05

TRNSYS – UNIVERSAL TOOL FOR CLIMATE ENGINEERING

TRANSSOLAR ENERGIETECHNIK

COMPLETION DATE
(SINCE 2007)

01 Street view. Foster & Partner's Masdar
   master plan for a carbon-neutral city
   in Abu Dhabi, United Arab Emirates, has
   been developed with Transsolar's universal tool for climate engineering.

02 Aerial view of the city.

02

ASSIGNMENT

Stuttgart-based climate engineers Transsolar are con-
cerned with more than energy conservation based upon
optimising thermal properties of the building envelope
and efficiency of technical equip-

CONCEPT

The success of
Transsolar's cli-
mate engineering
work is based on
the availability
of software tools
that can model
innovative energy
and climate con-
cepts. Thermal sim-
ulation is thus
mandatory for
concept valida-
tion, optimisation
and evaluation of
energy savings
and comfort. The
concepts enabled
by such simula-
tion have a huge
impact on the
architecture and
sustainability of
projects. ◣

ment. They seek a more holistic
design recognising the interdepen-
dence of factors affecting comfort
and integrating the functions of
architectural and technical equipment, such as daylight, natural
ventilation, air quality, air temperature, acoustics, and the well-
being of individuals. It is their
aim to minimise the building systems
and allow the architecture itself to
provide climate control. ◣

ENERGY CONCEPT

Numerous outstanding concepts illustrate the environmental and sustainable enhancement of the built environment even under extreme climate conditions due
to the continuous development of TRNSYS. The upcoming
release of TRNSYS 17 includes improved simulation of
highly glazed large spaces such as multi-story atriums. The existing multi-zone building model is extended
to allow detailed modelling of the thermal stratifica-
tion and complex radiation exchange that occur in these
spaces. In addition, further research is related to
comfort evaluation models that take into account solar
shortwave radiation. These types of continuous enhance-
ments enable engineers and researchers worldwide to vali-
date concepts ranging from simple solar domestic hot
water systems to passive low-energy buildings and their
equipment. ◣

REALISATION

Transsolar's primary thermal simulation tool is TRNSYS. It is a simulation environment for the
transient (e.g. hour-by-hour or minute-by-minute) simulation of thermal systems including multi-
zone buildings. Since the foundation of Transsolar in 1992 the company has focused on improving the
multi-zone building model of TRNSYS. This model includes the key building physics that are often
at the heart of our climate concepts. The multi-zone building model has integrated models for thermally activated slabs, capillary tube systems, chilled ceilings, human comfort and more. TRNSYS also
includes a large variety of detailed standard components and add-ons such as geothermal or airflow
models. Key to the power of TRNSYS is the flexibility provided by a modular and open structure,
which allows the integration of user-written components and even on-the-fly interaction with other
programmes. All of these features allow concepts such as double-skin façades, natural ventilation,
and active slabs to be represented with an accuracy that no other commercial software allows. ◣

ELM PARK LOW DEVELOPMENT
BUCHOLZ MCEVOY ARCHITECTS

ENGINEER
Transsolar Energietechnik, RFR Paris

CLIENT
Radora Developments Ltd. Dublin

PROJECT LOCATION
Dublin, Ireland

COMPLETION DATE
2008

01 The building frames are constructed primarily from concrete with timber from renewable sources for additional structure and cladding.

01 Most of the long-span structural elements are composed of glued laminated timber, engineered as supports for the breathing façades.

02 Cross section of the building illustrating the environmental concept.

ASSIGNMENT

The client's brief was to "achieve as much development on the site as possible" under sustainable conditions. ▶

CONCEPT

The solution for the brief was a miniature city of over 100,000 square metres. Elm Park is a low energy, high-density, mixed-use project con-sisting of a private hospital, hotel, offices, restaurant, crèche, conference centre, apartments and housing for senior citizens, as well as a leisure centre with pool along with cafés and sandwich bars all set in a richly landscaped, eight-hectare green public space. From the very beginning, the main idea was to minimise energy demand, maximise density, flexibility and mix of use while creating an elegant and expressive environment. The architects' intention was to achieve this by maximising the benefits of the buildings' orientation, form and shape, natural light and ventilation and by creating a large public landscape of water and green. ▶

LOCATION

The generator of the proposal was the opportunity to retain the site as a parkland setting, as a green lung for the city of Dublin. The compact footprint of the buildings allows for maximum green space and little obstruction to views across the Dublin mountains. The rich mix of use allows an ongoing 24-hour ebb and flow of life on the site. The urban landscape is enriched by creating a new web of routes, intersections and nodes on its surface. ▶

02

REALISATION

"This project offers the possibility of a new type of urban development in Dublin," says Bucholz McEvoy, "one which is firmly stitched into its natural environment, while fine-tuned to the energy conserving/generating and functional potential of its components." The development consists of a functionally diverse ensemble of elements integrated into a continuous, energy-balanced piece of urban landscape. Buildings are lifted off ground level, releasing it for use as a public garden and allowing the free flow of plants, animals, water, humans, air and light. Buildings are thin to allow natural light and ventilation. They are oriented on a north-south axis to give clear east and west elevations for maximum daylight and good views. The car park and site services are underground, yet naturally lit. Waste recycling is accommodated within the basement connected directly to all buildings. This means that a continuous garden covers the ground-floor level. The buildings define different areas with courtyards within the garden, each with individual characters, reference points and vistas.

The public concourse overlooking the gardens is the heart of the scheme, linking all the buildings and becoming a meeting place, business place and containing the communal facilities such as cafés and small bookshops. Entrances to the office buildings, hotel and hospital are directly off the concourse. The building frames are constructed primarily from concrete with timber from renewable sources for additional structure and cladding. Most of the long-span structural elements are composed of glued laminated timber, engineered as supports for the breathing façades. Glass is the primary external membrane which maximises daylight, controls heat gain and minimises heat loss. The residential buildings are clad in cedar timber. ▶

ENERGY CONCEPT

A very important consideration for the design was to achieve a resilient energy concept through maximising passive means, such as orientation of the buildings and pressure difference between inside and outside to create air movement, and active means such as the energy design, where complimentary functions were mixed. Minimising energy use, say the architects, is about minimising energy consumption through design of the built environment – by means of orientation, building height, width and employing the buildings' structure and façades as part of the ventilation strategy which harnesses the energy of the prevailing winds. Together these produce an environment which is physiologically balanced with the human need for comfort. The office buildings are climate-controlled without the use of mechanical ventilation or air conditioning. The buildings' large west-facing thin atria act as ventilation lungs, maintaining comfortable internal temperatures. The shared energy management strategy means that energy can be moved around according to demand: it can be used primarily during the day by offices and in the evenings by residences, with excess energy stored in the swimming pool. A combined heat and power plant turns heat energy into power to supply office needs. A wood pellet boiler supplies hot water for heating both apartments and offices. The development also has a seven-hectare green roof including over 500 trees, thousands of shrubs and grasses to encourage water and air quality recycling. ▶

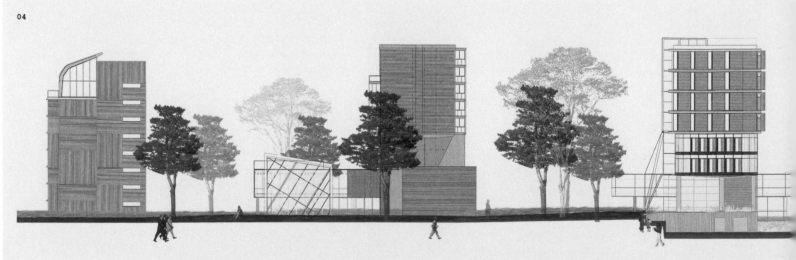

01 Buildings are lifted off ground level, releasing it for use as a public garden.

02 View from the water side.

03 Side view. The thin buildings allow natural light and ventilation.

04 Elevation of the development. The buildings define different areas with courtyards within the garden, each with individual characters, reference points and vistas.

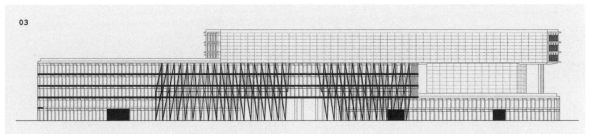

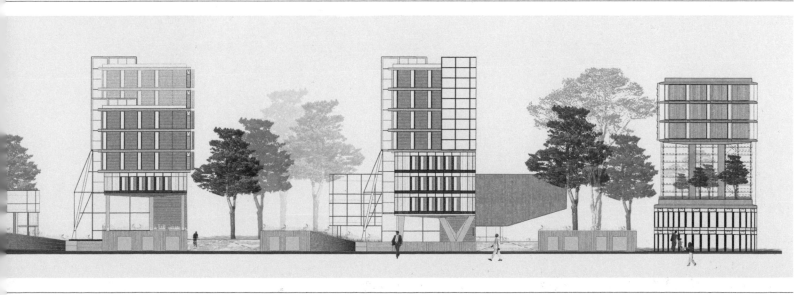

01 View from above. Elm Park is set in a richly
landscaped eight hectare green public space.

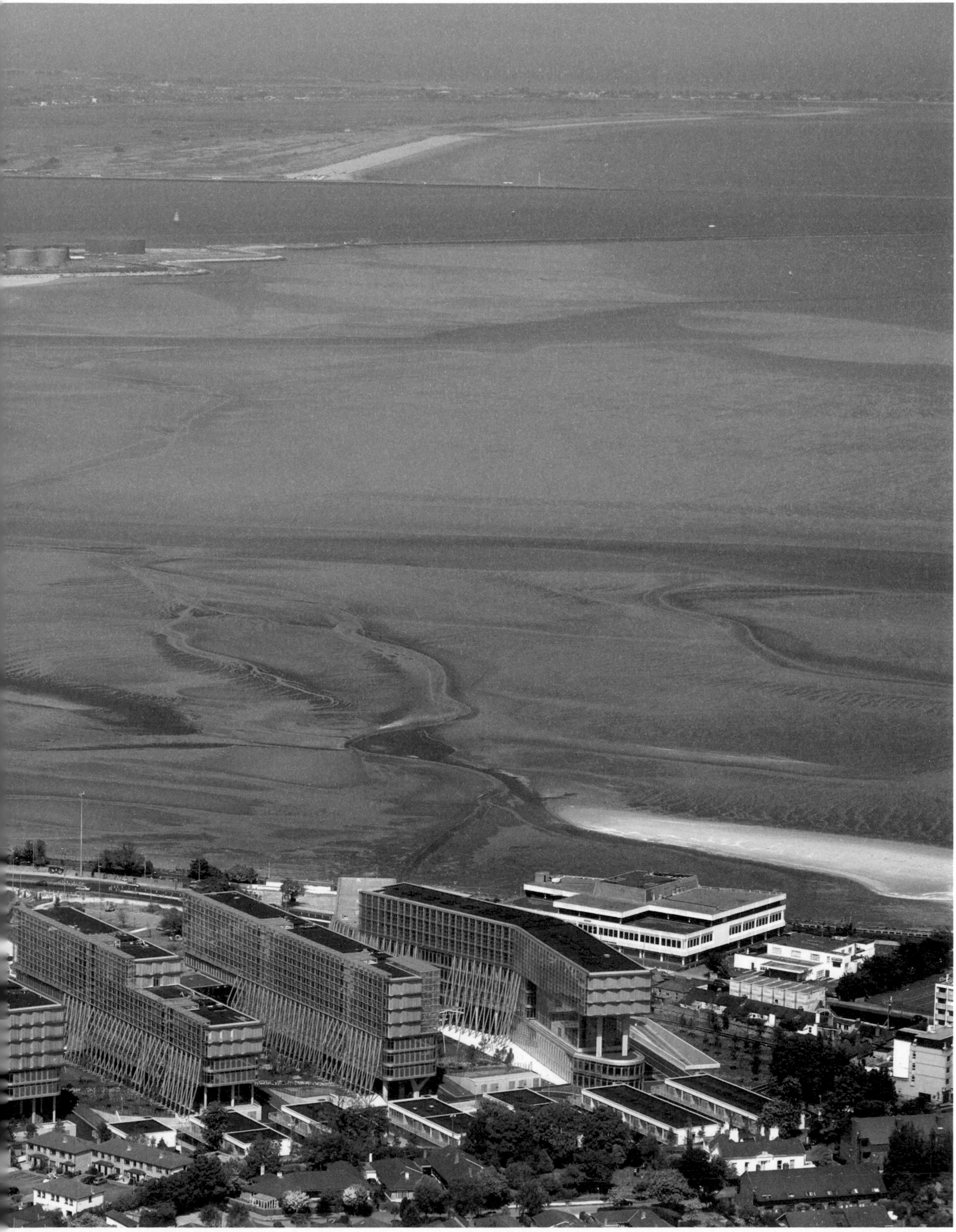

CONSULTANTS
Ove Arup &
Partners
(engineering and
sustainability);
Rutherford &
Chekene (civil
engineering)

CLIENT
California
Academy
of Sciences

PROJECT LOCATION
Golden Gate Park,
San Francisco, USA

COMPLETION DATE
2008

CALIFORNIA ACADEMY OF SCIENCES
RENZO PIANO BUILDING WORKSHOP

01 The roof as a living surface
with native Californian plants
and wild flowers.

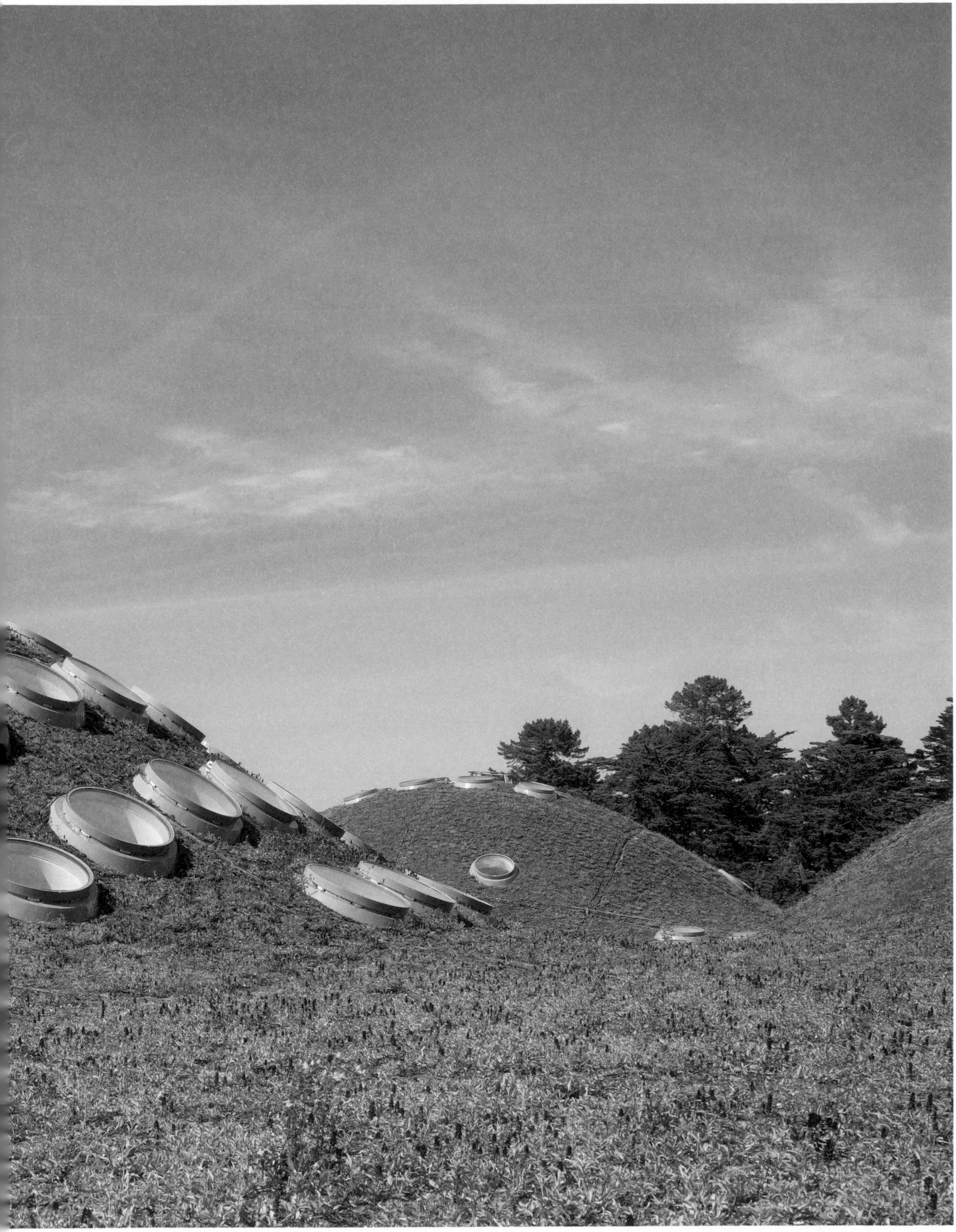

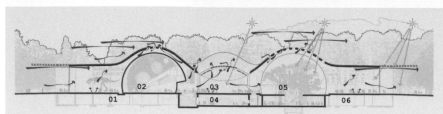

01 Section of the building illustrating
the environmental features.

01.01 Back of house.
01.02 Planetarium.
01.03 Piazza.
01.04 Aquarium exhibits.
01.05 Rain forest.
01.06 Back of house.

ASSIGNMENT

The project was assigned to the Renzo Piano Building Workshop after a series of interviews with architectural offices all over the world. The primary goal in building a new Academy was to provide a safe, modern facility for exhibition, education, conservation and research under one roof. The design should also reflect the building's role, housing one of the world's most innovative and prestigious scientific and cultural institutions. ▸

LOCATION

The California Academy of Sciences in San Francisco is one of the few natural science institutes where the public experience has been directly related to in-house scientific research, done in the same building, since its foundation. The new Academy is designed on the same site of the previous facility in Golden Gate Park. This project required the demolition of most of the 11 existing buildings, built between 1916 and 1976. ▸

CONCEPT

The mission statement of the Academy ("To explore, explain and protect the natural world") combined with the mild San Francisco climate made this project ideally suited for incorporating sustainable design strategies. In addition to energy-efficient heating and cooling, a more holistic approach was agreed upon, involving careful consideration in the choice of building products, recycling of the materials of the old Academy and the way in which they are put together. Integral to the building design are the location of spaces in relation to daylight and ventilation, the efficient use of water and run-off from the roof, as well as the generation of energy. Sustainability is also part of the exhibition design, the exhibition philosophy, and its day-to-day operation. As a functioning demonstration, the public will be able to see and understand many of the principles of sustainable design. ▸

ENERGY CONCEPT

The Academy's "Living Roof" is a natural insulation layer that is around four degrees Celsius cooler than a standard roof. Rainwater is partially absorbed in a special layer, creating a water reservoir for growing plants. The remaining rainwater is collected and used to flush toilets. The roof absorbs up to 3.6 million gallons of water per year, preventing run-off from carrying pollutants into the ecosystem. It provides excellent insulation, keeping interior temperatures about ten degrees cooler. The build-up and materials used include biodegradable coconut husk trays containing soil and species of Californian plants, an erosion-control blanket design to retain soil, a drainage layer, an insulation layer, a waterproof layer and a concrete slab. The edge of the roof (the canopy) is filled with photovoltaic cells in a sandwich of glass. These cells will produce five to ten per cent of the electricity needs of the building. The building has 30 per cent less energy consumption than the federal code requires, and 90 per cent of office space will have natural light and ventilation. The ten-metre-high flexible exhibit space under the roof on the ground level benefits from natural light and ventilation through the façades and the roof. The space is ventilated by means of operable vents in the glazed façades and openings at the large undulations of the roof, where warmer air is allowed to escape during the day, while the shape of the roof pulls the warm air out of the building. Care was taken with the selection of materials for the buildings and minimising waste: 90 per cent of all demolition materials from the previous buildings was recycled, 95 per cent of all steel was from recycled sources, 50 per cent of lumber was harvested from sustainable-yield forests and 68 per cent of insulation came from recycled blue jeans. Recycled denim insulation holds more heat and absorbs sound better than spun fibreglass insulation. It is also safer to handle. Even when denim insulation is treated with fire retardants and fungicides to prevent mildew, it is still easier to work with and does not require installers to wear protective clothing or respirators. During the cold season, the Academy is heated by a radiant heat system of hot water pipes embedded in the floor. This keeps heat close to where it is needed - close to the occupants - and reduces the building's energy needs by some ten per cent annually in comparison to an air-forced system. The building has a platinum LEED rating. ▸

REALISATION

The new building retains the former Academy's location and orientation, and like the original Academy, all functions are organised around a central piazza, or courtyard. A sophisticated system of retractable fabric screens for sun, rain and acoustics are important features that help to control microclimates in this space.

Three historic elements of the previous Academy have been maintained in some fashion, as a link to the past: the African Hall, the North American (California) Hall and the entrance to the Steinhart Aquarium. Two spherical exhibits, the Planetarium Dome and the Rainforest Biosphere, are located adjacent to the piazza. Together with the reconstructed entrance of the Steinhart Aquarium, these elements represent the Academy: Space, Earth and Ocean. These three icons push the roof up, creating the undulating roofscape called the "Living Roof". Floating at the same height as that of the original halls, the new roof formally unifies the institute. It is landscaped with native plant species that are drought resistant and do not require irrigation once established. The roof extends beyond the perimeter walls and becomes a glass canopy providing shade, protection from the rain, and generates energy through photovoltaic cells in the glass. In the centre of the "Living Roof" a glazed skylight covers the piazza. Much smaller skylights distributed over the surface of the roof allow natural light into the exhibit space and can be opened automatically for natural ventilation of the space below. ▸

02 The Rainforest Bio-
sphere. The entire
building serves as
a sort of specimen
case, a framework
for pondering the
natural world while
straining to disturb
it as little as
possible.

01 Top view of green roof with its bubbles.

02 View of the entrance situation.

03 Technical drawing of bubble with skylights.

04 Longitudinal elevation of the building.

05 A bubble containing a rain-forest habitat.

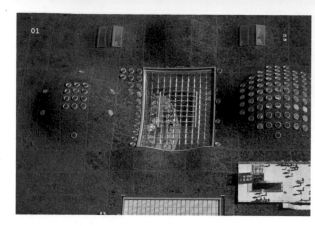

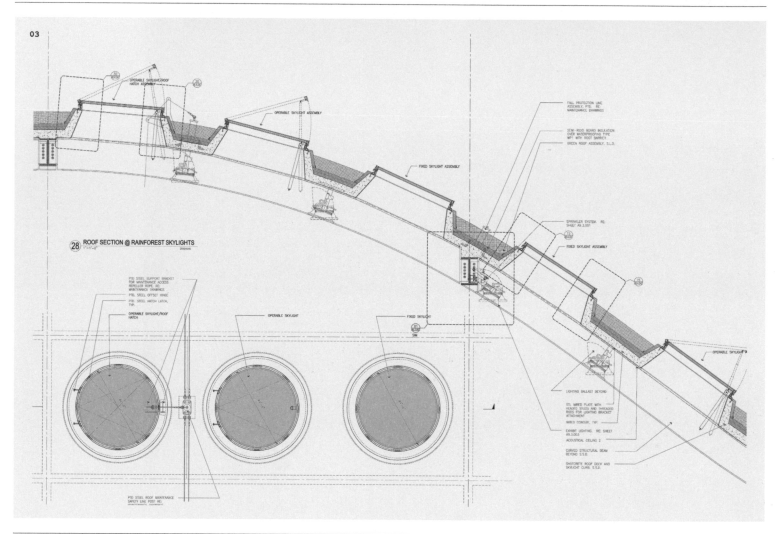

28 ROOF SECTION @ RAINFOREST SKYLIGHTS

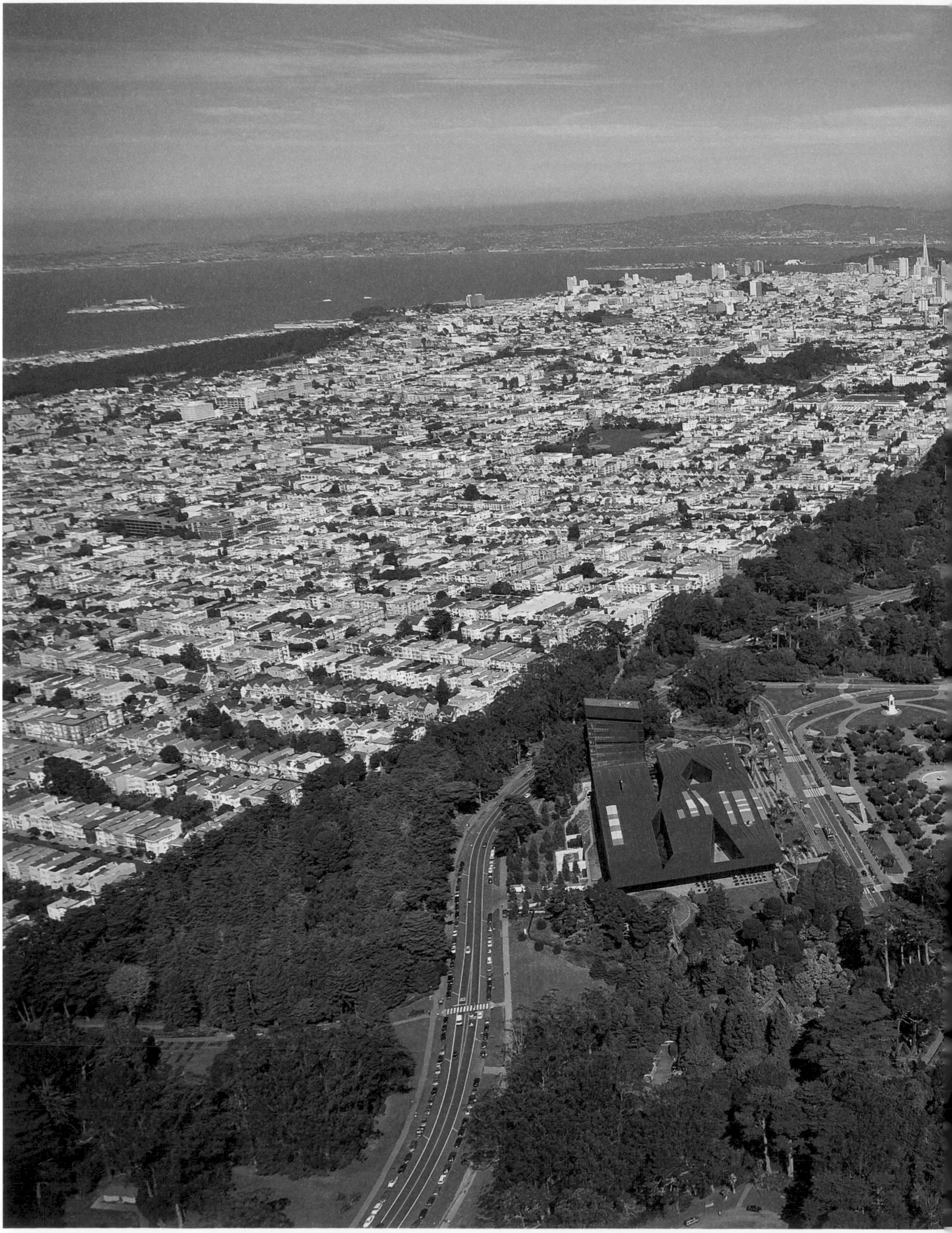

01 The California Academy of Sciences in San Francisco is designed on the same site of the previous facility in Golden Gate Park. The building's green roof is now the largest swath of native vegetation in the city.

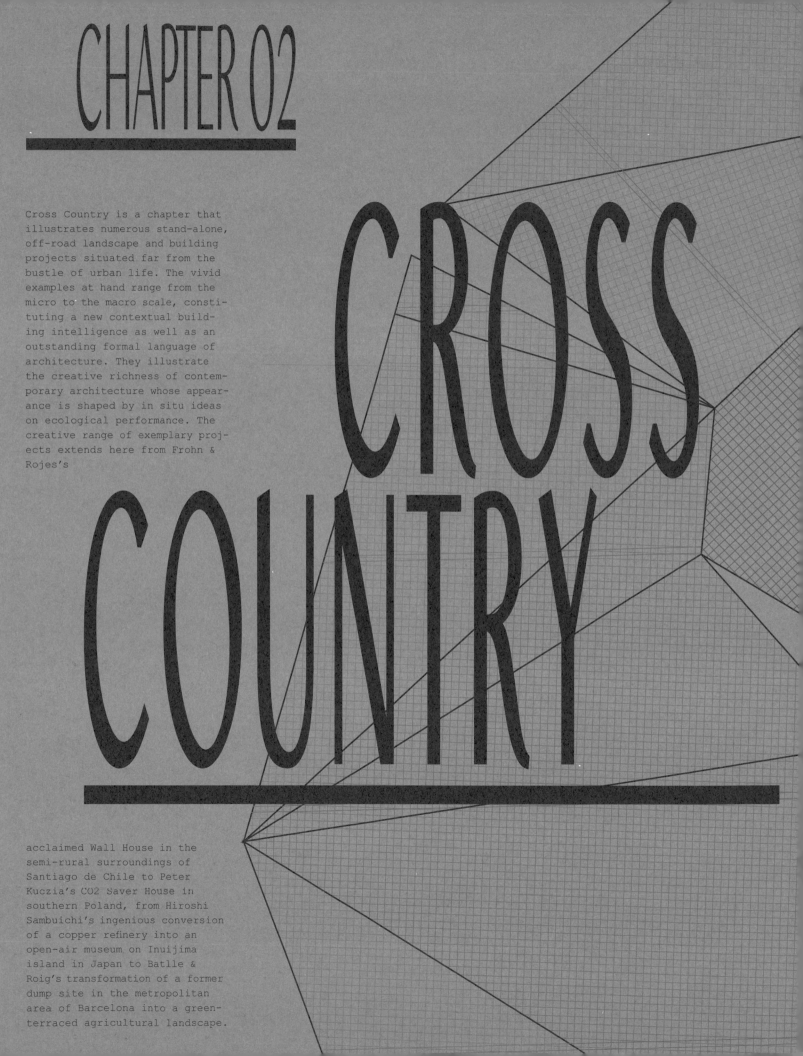

CHAPTER 02

Cross Country is a chapter that illustrates numerous stand-alone, off-road landscape and building projects situated far from the bustle of urban life. The vivid examples at hand range from the micro to the macro scale, constituting a new contextual building intelligence as well as an outstanding formal language of architecture. They illustrate the creative richness of contemporary architecture whose appearance is shaped by in situ ideas on ecological performance. The creative range of exemplary projects extends here from Frohn & Rojes's

CROSS COUNTRY

acclaimed Wall House in the semi-rural surroundings of Santiago de Chile to Peter Kuczia's CO2 Saver House in southern Poland, from Hiroshi Sambuichi's ingenious conversion of a copper refinery into an open-air museum on Inuijima island in Japan to Batlle & Roig's transformation of a former dump site in the metropolitan area of Barcelona into a green-terraced agricultural landscape.

LUKAS FEIREISS IN CONVERSATION WITH PETER SLOTERDIJK PART 2

DYNAMIC DWEL-LING IN THE AGE OF FIREWORKS

LF: Certainly Werner Sobek ranks among the international pioneers of consistently ecologically intelligent architecture. Purely with regard to their formal idiom, however, his buildings – in terms of their inner and outer transparency and engineering clarity – stand very much in the tradition of modernist architecture. Interestingly, many of the bolder experiments with the formal idiom in contemporary architecture are nowadays informed just as crucially by the efficiency of their ecological performance. As a member of the international, interdisciplinary jury for the Zumtobel Group Awards for Sustainability and Humanity in the Built Environment in 2007, you helped select prize-winners and runners-up from among the roughly 40 projects submitted. What did you learn from that experience?

PS: I was most impressed by the incredible surplus of intelligence articulated by all these designs by engineers and architects. When you see what these people have already thought up, our ordinary built reality seems several orders of magnitude more stupid. There is clearly an enormous deficit in transfer and implementation. It is tempting to say that the solutions are already there but the problems haven't noticed it yet. For that reason, the time spent with the designs submitted for the Zumtobel Award inspired me enormously. The many projects for humanitarian initiatives that you presented made me think of the concept of "emergency design" developed by Yana Milev – a new concept for an architecture of states of exception. For me, as a theorist of moving, these designs were as instructive as they were stimulating. ▶

LF: The jury was composed of experts from a wide variety of disciplines. What do you see as the advantages and disadvantages of thinking and working in an interdisciplinary way?

PS: I have been considering for some time how to overcome the self-imposed ignorance of the humanities with respect to the rapid progress of research in the natural sciences. My concern results in no small measure from my efforts to establish a general immunology and to show how it effortlessly transcends the boundary between organisms and societies. I am sometimes annoyed by the stupidity of those colleagues who immediately scream "biologism" as soon as one uses a biological concept such as immune system in the context of theories of culture. Most of them are not even aware that the concept of immunity was

at home in legal studies for two millennia before scientists borrowed it. Not infrequently, it is biologists who borrow from us, not just the other way around. Take the concept of the cell, for example. It was originally an architectural metaphor that was spread by the modern technology of the microscope. When the British physicist Robert Hooke first observed a piece of cork under a microscope in the seventeenth century, he was astonished by the regularity of the spatial patterns, which reminded him of the arrangement of cells in a monastery. That was how the concept of the cell moved from the theory of architecture to biology – and no one raised the alarm. Similarly with immune systems: the legal, ritual/symbolic, and architectural forms of securing existence by means of immunisation had been in common use long before biologists came up with the idea that organisms have anything like an immune system.

In the context of our topic, all of this demonstrates that even such primary sciences as biology – which is at the centre of our natural sciences these days – is permeated by problems relating to the theory of space. Talk to biologists today, and you'll discover that they're all on this topological trip. Recently, I spoke to an embryologist who, as part of a special lecture to open the new semester in Karlsruhe, presented images of original phytogenesis after the fertilisation of an ovum. Professor Wittbrod's lecture was nothing less than an introduction to topological mysteries, since he spoke of primitive symmetries and the development of a body axis, and of the start of a unique building activity around this axis by the nascent embryo. It gave the impression that a good biologist will, by virtue of his métier, willingly or unwillingly become something like a proto-architect, who sees spontaneous formations of space in nature and is more or less speechless about everything that happens there, and how it happens. By the way, Buckminster Fuller's notion of tensegrity migrated to cellular biology and has served as a model with a great deal of descriptive power with regard to natural phenomena, despite the fact that some observers of Fuller's structures initially may have felt that they were merely the hybrid games of an engineer who had grown bored with classical statics, with the old game of wall, load and pillar. In the meanwhile, however, we know that cells have always worked with post-classical statics; much of nature thinks in Fullerian categories. ▶

I HAVE BEEN CONSIDERING FOR SOME TIME, HOW TO OVERCOME THE SELF-IMPOSED IGNORANCE OF THE HUMANITIES WITH RESPECT TO THE RAPID PROGRESS OF RESEARCH IN THE NATURAL SCIENCES

IT IS A CULTURE OF WASTE AND ATMOSPHERIC RECKLESSNESS, A WAY OF LIFE THAT IS BASED ON CONSTANT FIREWORKS. THE NEXT ARCHITEC-TURE WILL HAVE TO BE AN ARCHITECTURE OF AT-MOSPHERIC RESPECT AND ECOLOGICAL RESTRAINT

LF: The present volume attempts to compile forward-looking examples of ecologically intelligent thinking and action in the built environment. For some time, we have known that the destruction of our natural bases for life and its consequences are among the great challenges of the twenty-first century. But it seems as if this information has only now truly arrived – its significance and scope only know fully grasped. How do you explain the sudden, almost ecstatic alarmism that characterises discussion of climate change and sustainability?

PS: The great project for the twenty-first century has been obvious for some time: foremost on the agenda is using technology to make a CO2-neutral civilisation possible. The intelligence of future engineers will have to prove itself on this front. In the language of the scientists who recently released the St. James's Palace Memorandum, that means simply the "decarbonisation of civilisation". Everyone immediately understands that is an epochal undertaking. Over a period of more than two centuries, we created a culture based on fossil fuels, and its principles have begun to totter. It is a culture of waste and atmospheric recklessness, a way of life that is based on constant fireworks. The next architecture will have to be an architecture of atmospheric respect and ecological restraint. In other words, we have to repeal the entire culture of fireworks. That – no more and no less – is the great difficulty we face. We are in essence all children of this pyromaniacal age; we have grown accustomed to living with an unbelievably high level of daily waste. We have even internalised our "right to waste things" and view that as the solid core of human rights. In that respect, an enormous retraining of our everyday habits will have to take place, and the most

important trainers and teachers on that front will be architects. To a certain extent, they have already begun to create new ways of living and new forms of housing appropriate to the new imperative. The other mega-task will be to design a corresponding form of mobility for the post-fossil-fuel age. In the future, we shall have to consider the two things together: dwelling and being on the move. Both of them place high demands on our technical intelligence. The architects of tomorrow can only do their job well if automobile designers working at other drafting tables do their job well. If I want to build a hotel in Abu Dhabi that conforms to the future demands for sustainable architecture, then sooner or later I need some invisible colleague who will design a vehicle that is impossible today: namely, an environmentally friendly aeroplane. For the foreseeable future, that appears to be the technical equivalent of squaring the circle – a problem that is too difficult for today's engineering intelligence. No one knows yet how large-scale aviation can exist without destroying the environment. An entirely new form of propulsion other than ruinous jet technology would have to be developed. The same is true of other areas of motorised travel, especially ship travel, which has long since urgently needed to emancipate itself from the perverse diesel engines on which navigation on the world's seas still depends – technologically, probably the most cynical form of environmental crime conceivable. The kilometre-long black filth that streams out of the smokestacks of ships on the high seas has to be seen to appreciate what these enormous fleets on the ocean are doing every day. It is truly a doomsday technology – and one about which people on land generally don't have a clue. ◤

LF: In light of the fact that cities are responsible for 75 per cent of carbon dioxide pollution and about half of the world's energy consumption is related to buildings, even the smallest construction project always turns out to be a little bit of architectural responsibility. Will our future perhaps be decided on urban terrain?

PS: The most important part of the struggle for a CO2-neutral civilisation will be fought on urban terrain. Most city dwellers today do not even realise that they live in an ecological impossibility; all they know is a life of constant urban fireworks. Indeed, most urban dwellers today consider themselves poor devils and live in hope of being able to really go all out in the future. Yet the truth, also for them, is that there is no avoiding the agenda for the age beyond fossil-fuel illusions. ▶

LF: The subject of your latest book, *Du musst Dein Leben ändern* (You must change your life), is the transformation that the crisis demands. The title of our book also refers to change: *Architecture of Change*. What kind of change is your book about?

PS: The title of my book is taken from a famous poem by Rainer Maria Rilke, in the final line of which there suddenly appears this strong imperative, "Du musst Dein Leben ändern". I proceed from this modern finding to a series of historical metamorphoses of this phrase, all of which demonstrate that for three millennia the ethical elites of high cultures have been living under excessive tensions that result from the need for a total reform of life. I go so far as to assert that the history of high culture is nothing but a long line of people who have taken the imperative "You must change your life" literally, and read it according to the circumstances of their time, as Brahmans, Buddhists, Stoics, Christians, aestheticians, politicians. In today's situation, "You must change your life" means that the old model for civilisation of Western, now global, industrial culture has to be turned completely upside down and replaced by something entirely new. This can be thought of as a spiritual requirement but also as pragmatic advice. There is no need to create a new religion to dissuade us from ecological suicide. The absolute imperative of our time demands an ethos and a technology compatible with the advanced state of cosmopolitan, ecological consciousness. ▶

THERE IS NO NEED TO CREATE A NEW RELIGION TO DISSUADE US FROM ECOLOGICAL SUICIDE

CO2 SAVER HOUSE

PETER KUCZIA

CLIENT
Peter & Dorota Kuczia

PROJECT LOCATION
Lake Laka, Poland

COMPLETION DATE:
2008

ASSIGNMENT

Subsidised by the German Federal Environmental Foundation in Osnabrück, this private house has been put into practice as an example of knowledge transfer on simple and cost-effective sustainable building practices from Germany to Poland and other East European countries.

LOCATION

The CO2 Saver House is located in the rural landscape of southern Poland near Lake Laka. ◣

CONCEPT

The design of the project was determined by the twin goals of low lifecycle costs and a reduction in construction costs. All details are simple, but well thought out. Cost-savings were made by applying traditional building techniques and using local materials and recycled building elements. For this reason, the house did not cost more than a conventional one in Poland. ◣

REALISATION

Using untreated larch wood and black fibre cement panels to optimise solar energy gain, this lake house in Poland is a good example of how to be sustainable and respectful to the environment. The house - like a chameleon - blends with its surroundings. Colourful planks within the timber façade reflect the tones of the rural landscape. The window reveals, with fibre cement cladding, frame images of the countryside. The building is on the outside symmetrical, while the internal zones are arranged asymmetrically according to function. ◣

ENERGY CONCEPT

The built form is designed to optimise the absorbance of solar energy. Approximately 80 per cent of the building envelope is facing a southerly direction. The single storey living space on the ground floor is externally clad with untreated larch boarding. Solar energy is trapped there by the set-in glazed patio. Solar collection panels are located on the roof, and a photovoltaic system is planned for the future. The dark façade of the "black box" - a three storey structure clad with charcoal-coloured fibre cement panels - is warmed by the sun, reducing heat loss to the environment. The passive and active solar energy concepts and a high standard of thermal insulation are enhanced by a ventilation plant with a thermal recovery system. The house consumes only about one tenth of the average used in a standard single-family house in Poland. ◣

01 View of the green roof.

02 Side view. The colourful planks within the timber façade reflect the tones of the countryside.

03 Front view. The built form optimises the absorption of solar energy.

04 Interior spaces are illuminated by natural light.

05 Floor plans and elevations of the building.

01

02

03

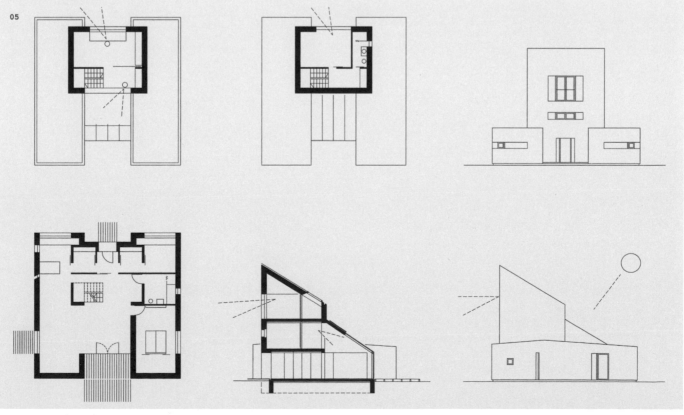

05

WALL HOUSE
FAR FROHN AND ROJAS: MARC FROHN, MARIO ROJAS TOLEDO

ENGINEER
Mario Wagner, Santiago de Chile (lumber)
Ernesto Villalon, Santiago de Chile(concrete)

CLIENT
Patricia Krause

PROJECT LOCATION
Santiago de Chile, Chile

COMPLETION DATE
2007

01/02 Views of the building that is half house, half tent.

01   02   03

ASSIGNMENT

FAR's Marc Frohn and Mario Rojas Toledo were asked to design a very affordable home for a young Chilean couple. The home was required to offer the clients both spaciousness within the house as well as visibility to the exterior in order to profit from the Chilean climate and the panorama of the Andean mountain range. After a series of talks, the architects and the clients agreed on a solution that would combine the clients' desire for a strong link to nature and the budgetary limitations into an innovative climate concept for a house which would not only minimise the running cost for their new home over the years, but also tie their living environment intimately with the surrounding environment. ◤

LOCATION

The building is situated in the semi-rural surroundings of Santiago de Chile, a rapidly developing hybrid of suburbia and agricultural hinterland. It is an area characterised by large, open lots, each isolated by tall hedges and rows of trees. ◤

CONCEPT

The result is a structure, half house, half tent, characterised by a series of four delaminated wall-layers (concrete cave, stacked shelving, milky shell, soft skin), between which the different inhabitable spaces of the house slip, creating a gradual transition between interior and exterior, providing views to the distant mountains of the Andes. The layering logic of the building unites architectural and environmental concepts, allowing a series of different climate zones to emerge. Moving from room to room plays with a perception of moving deeper or shallower, with changes of materiality and lighting providing a range of qualitative experiences and cues. ◤

REALISATION

The various building layers are carefully adjusted to both the production economy of mostly untrained local labour and a very tight budget of 100,000 euros. While the innermost zones contain the most demanding functions associated with the home (i.e. bathroom and kitchen), the selection of materials roughens up towards the exterior. An introverted concrete core that forms the first element of the structural system contains the house's two bathrooms. Surrounding the inner core is a pair of upper and lower structural shelving bands, built of engineered wood, formwork panels and plywood that set up varying configurations for the placement of domestic articles, privacy or openness, and levels of illumination according to programme and orientation. Moving out to the climate threshold, an upwardly folding translucent skin, or milky shell, of high-insulation UV-filtering multi-layered polycarbonate panels provides protection from the harsh Chilean sun. The skin registers shadows of trees and outside elements on its surface and floods the zone with light. Two surfaces of the envelope are fully double-glazed. They contain full-height sliding doors, which – depending on the time of day and season – allow a complete opening toward the exterior and for the breeze to enter. Finally, a soft fabric membrane, typically not used in residential architecture but instead in greenhouse environments, acts as an energy screen, reflecting up to 75 per cent of the solar energy reaching the building, and at the same time creating a protective barrier against mosquitoes and insects. Wrapping itself entirely around the house, this soft casing creates a tent-like screened porch between inside and out, fully open to breezes and varyingly open to views, yet still providing a protective sheath. ◤

ENERGY CONCEPT

The project carefully combines local construction knowledge and at the same time introduces few imported materials (a polycarbonate and energy screen), which were selected for their environmental performance. Through the spatial and material configuration of the individual wall layers, the project develops an appropriate architectural approach to deal with the local climate (summer between 30 and 35 degrees Celsius, winter up to 10 degrees Celsius). All wood products used in the house have been grown, felled and processed around Arauco, Chile. The shelving bands have been prefabricated in a local furniture factory. With its separated wall layers, the project unites architectural and energy concepts. The individual wall layers do not only build upon one another geometrically, but in the context of the energy concept establish a finely calibrated hierarchy between one another. The concrete core and the ground floor concrete slab contain gas-powered radiant heating. The ground floor is climatised by the slab, while the concrete core radiates heat into the open-plan second floor space. For that purpose, PEX-hoses are integrated into the concrete elements. During the summer, the circuit can be appropriated for passive cooling using a heat pump. In this case, the water in the PEX-serpentines is cooled to 15 degrees Celsius. The cooling of the component needs far less energy than conventional air conditioning systems. ◤

01 Moving from room to room, changes in materiality and lighting provide a range of qualitative experiences.

02 A soft fabric membrane acts as an energy screen and protective barrier against prevalent mosquitoes and insects.

03 Full-height sliding doors allow a complete opening toward the exterior.

04 Introverted concrete core and shelving system.

05 View of one of the two bathrooms.

06 The fully double-glazed envelope of the building.

05

04

06

01

02/03/04

01 View of study model of the Wall House.

02 View of concrete cave and ground-floor shelving.

03 View of stacked shelving.

04 View of milky shell.

05 Rendering of building with soft skin.

06 Various conceptual models.

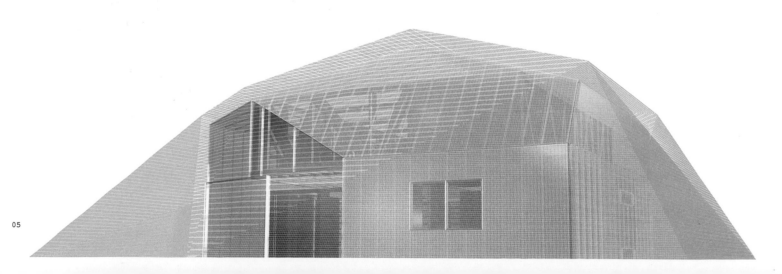

05

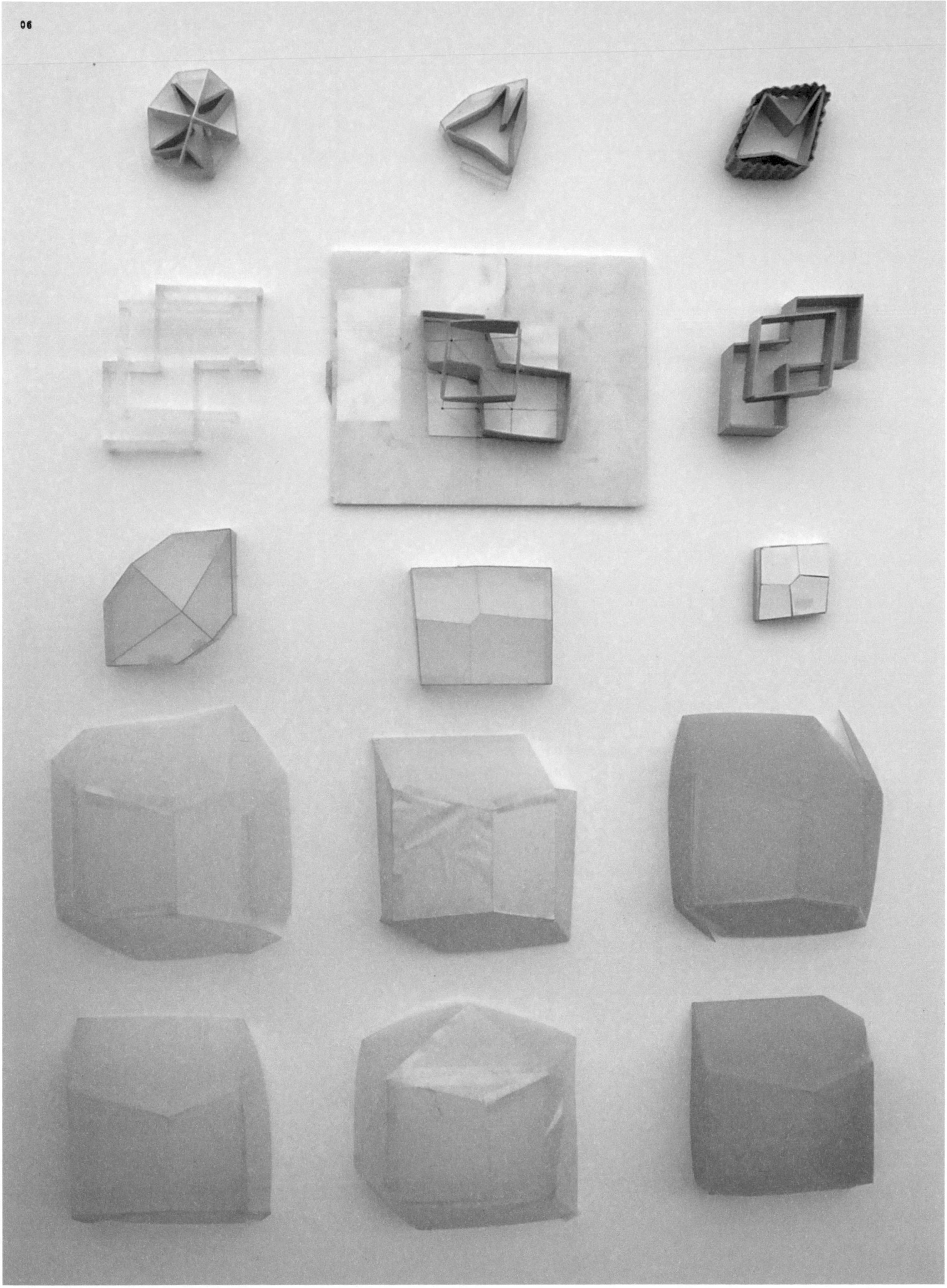

SOLAR HOUSE: SOLAR DECATHLON 07 TEAM DEUTSCHLAND
STUDENTS FROM THE DARMSTADT UNIVERSITY OF TECHNOLOGY (WITH PROF. MANFRED HEGGERNAU)

CLIENT
U.S. Department of Energy

PROJECT LOCATION
Darmstadt / Germany
Washington D.C. / USA
Essen / Germany
Stuttgart / Germany

COMPLETION DATE
2007

01 View of the building at one of it's many locations.

02 The louvers provide shade and privacy as well as generating energy via integrated photovoltaic cells.

01

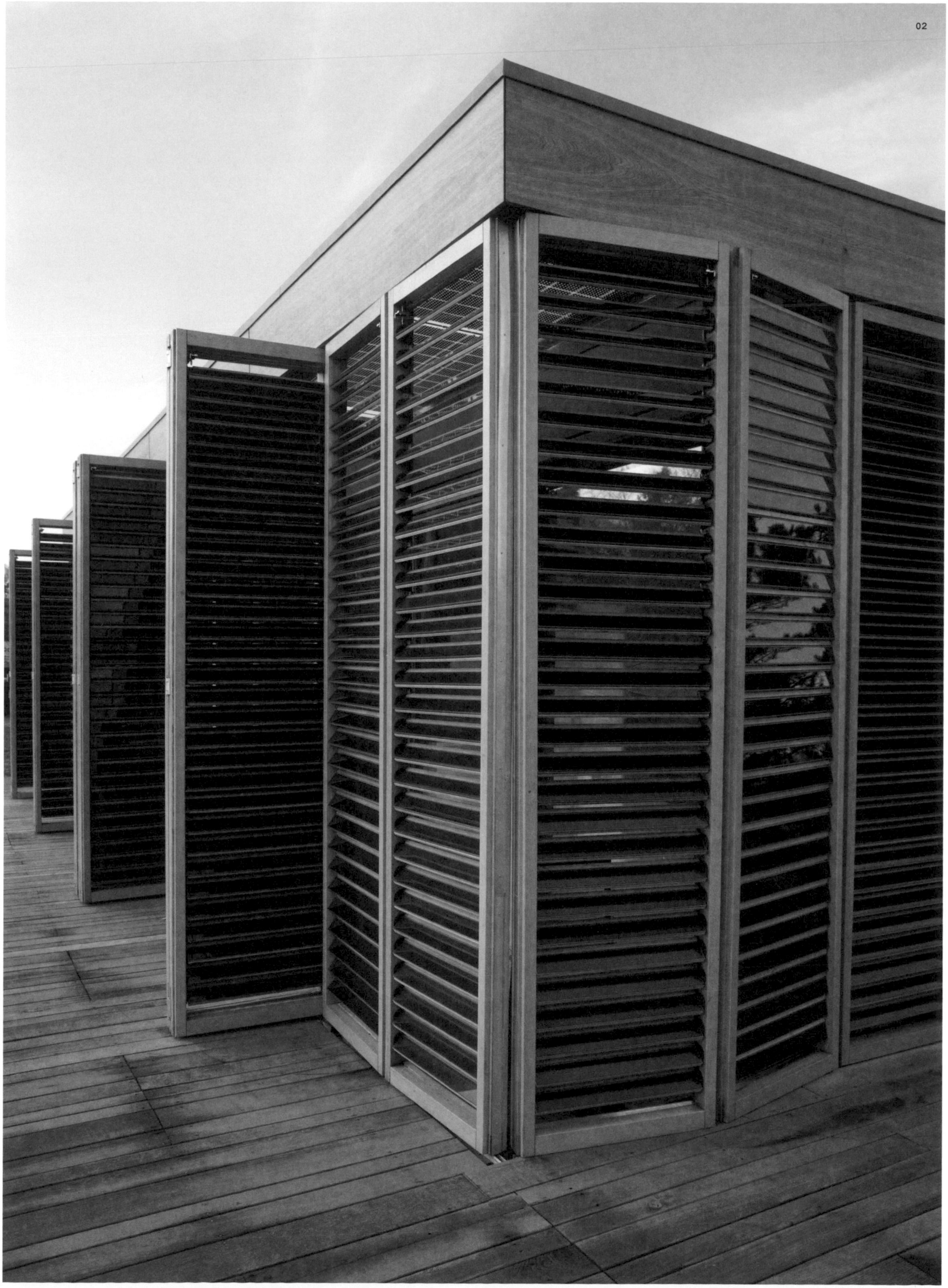

CONCEPT

The team wanted to reduce energy demand without losing comfort and, of course, the complete energy system had to be regenerative. The future homeowners should not just save money on fuel bills but also help reduce global warming and environmental pollution. They could even make money by selling excess electricity (made by the sun). The combination of aesthetics, comfort and technology was an important consideration. The house was designed for a young, two-person household. It was designed to provide maximal comfort along with minimal energy use, maximised energy gains and aesthetically pleasing architecture. The design concept for the house was based on three principles:

01) Layers

Like an onion, two layers were arranged around a central core. The outer layer provided shade, power generation and protection from the weather, while the inner layer provided insulation. Both layers combined several functions, such as shading and electricity generation, and they were variable to adjust the house to the users' demands according to time of day and season.

02) Platform

The house sat on an elevated double floor, called the 'platform', which contained the technical installation and storage space as well as integrated, exchangeable and stow-away furniture.

03) Open space

Apart from a central core containing kitchen and private facilities, the house had no separate mono-functional rooms. It was flexible and adjustable to serve different functions. ◣

ASSIGNMENT

The assignment was to create a house (for the year 2015) which should work completely off the grid – just by solar power. The footprint had to be maximum of 800 square feet. Twenty teams were selected by the U.S. Department of Energy to compete in the 2007 Solar Decathlon. The teams, from colleges and universities around the globe, participated in a competition to design, build and operate the most attractive and energy-efficient solar-powered home. The teams installed their solar houses on the National Mall in Washington, D.C., where they formed a solar village. The competition covered ten areas: architecture, engineering, communication and documentation, appliances, market viability, comfort zone, hot water, lighting, energy balance and getting around to determine an overall winner. Using only energy from the sun, the teams generated enough electricity to run a modern household. The students also chose the systems, products and appliances used in their houses. The 07 team from the Darmstadt University of Technology were the overall winners of the competition. ◣

ENERGY CONCEPT

Transparency is an important factor for the building. The façade featured large-sized windows and was still highly insulated. The façade had six floor-to-ceiling window elements on either side. All windows featured insulated oak frames. Four elements of the northern façade were quadruple-glazed. Two elements of the northern façade, including the front door and the ventilation opening, consisted of oak façade panels, highly insulated with vacuum insulation. This combination prevented heat loss and still allowed a mostly transparent northern façade. All south-facing façade elements were triple-glazed.

Energy conservation was as important a consideration as energy generation. Therefore walls, floor and ceiling were insulated with six-centimetre-thick vacuum insulation panels with a moisture barrier towards the inside, achieving an equivalent insulation value of about 60 centimetres of conventional insulation. Due to the low panel thickness, neither insulation nor clearance had to be compromised. The ventilation system featured a heat recovery unit, which recovered outgoing heat and reused it for the climatisation of the incoming fresh air. The remaining heat energy in the waste air was used to run a heat pump for the domestic hot water, boosted by two solar thermal collectors. In cooler climates the fresh air would be sucked in through a pipe running through the earth, so it could be cooled down in summer and warmed up in winter. Because the house has a light wooden structure, there is very little thermal mass inside the structure, which could lead to overheating in summertime. Therefore the interior walls and ceiling were clad in gypsum with phase-change material inside. This micro-capsulated paraffin absorbed energy by means of chemical phase change (e.g. solid to fluid) and re-emitted this energy as the ambient temperature dropped. The interior ceiling panels also contained a layer of matted capillary tubes, which could carry water. The capillary circuit led through a cool water storage tank, integrated into the platform. At night, the water in the tank was pumped up and sprayed over the roof then re-collected and stored in the tank. Thus the heat collected in the ceiling during the day was transferred to the cooling tank by the water in the capillary circuit, prolonging the effectiveness of the phase-change material. The louvred façade consisted of 48 frames with louvres that tracked the sun automatically (using specially developed software) and provided shade. ◣

REALISATION

The entire house was built by a team of 25 students on the campus of the Darmstadt University of Technology. It had a post-and-beam construction made from locally resourced wood from regenerative forestry. The main load-bearing structure was made from fir, fortified with steel inserts for transport and lifting. The stiffening and sheeting consisted of beach-plywood and so-called Livingboards. Livingboards are chipboards, manufactured from waste wood from wood production using formaldehyde-free glues. Oak was used for all visible columns and surfaces. The modern handling and language of form provided an opportunity to clean up the cliché of German oak. Everything could be covered and closed-up to floor level, so the space above could be used differently. Also integrated were technical installations such as electrical conduits, duct-works and pipes. All could be accessed through openings from above. The core of the house contained the kitchen and the bathroom. Its shell was of translucent acrylic and had a matte surface. As the technical heart of the building, the core also contained the building systems. Besides the kitchen and bath installations, it bundled the HVAC and hot water systems, as well as electricity controls. Comfort, accessibility and functional design were guiding aspects in selecting the plumbing and lighting fixtures. Integrated LED lighting enabled the core to glow and underlined its physical presence. ◣

01

02

01 Storage space and bulky furniture, such as the bed and sofa, were integrated into the double floor to maximise the footprint.

02 View towards the kitchen.

03 The roof above the porch consists of two glass panels with photovoltaic cells in between. It protects the user from rain and sun and generates electricity at the same time.

04 Design and lines of furniture and lighting systems followed function and simple elegance, consisting of long-lasting, possibly renewable materials, providing timeless sustainability.

04

YAKISUGI HOUSE

LANDSCAPE DESIGN
Terunobu Fujimori + Akira Koyama

CLIENT
Private

PROJECT LOCATION
Nagano City, Nagano Prefecture, Japan

COMPLETION DATE
2007

TERUNOBU FUJIMORI + KEICHI KAWAKAMI

01 A small hut-like building in the surrounding garden serves as a place to rest.

02 External walls are covered with highly durable charred cedar boards.

01 The planks are charcoaled on one side, creating a distinctive and unusual surface.

02 Trees grow through the copper roof structure.

03 The living and dining room are inspired by small cave dwellings.

04 Small narrow doorways lead to the connecting rooms.

05 Internal walls are clad in chestnut boards and plaster.

02/03

01

04

05

ASSIGNMENT

A two-storey, residential wooden construction, with landscaped garden in the Nagano district of Japan. ▶

CONCEPT

"In the architectural world," says architect Terunobu Fujimori, "ecology and sustainability have been and are mostly a matter of energy conversion and building materials. This is, of course, very important, but architectural expression is my top priority and sustainability is a matter of architectural expression. The role of an architect is, I think, to put together every possible element into a single complete work and give one expression." Fujimori seeks to pursue the most suitable architectural expression of ecology and sustainability by taking natural materials such as sand, wood, stone and grass and using them in a manner that is as natural as possible. Unlike industrial materials, natural materials are characterised by inequality and irregularity, and Fujimori tries to bring out this uniqueness. His approach to each of his buildings is not limited by a particular mode of expression, or style, originating in any one country or era. This is because nature itself, which is the model for ecology and sustainability, "has neither national nor historical differentiation". The Yakisugi House was in part inspired by a small cave dwelling near the Caves of Lascaux in France, which Fujimori encountered on his travels. The cave feeling is reflected in the wood-clad living and dining area, which leads on through small narrow doorways to a study, two bedrooms and a tearoom inside a mini tower perched on the edge of the building's highest point. ▶

LOCATION

The Yakisugi House was planned for a local city area where wooden materials are abundant. The structure and finishing are made entirely from local wood. ▶

REALISATION

The external walls are covered with highly durable charred cedar boards – a traditional Japanese cladding material. The planks are charcoaled on one side to a depth of one centimetre, which increases durability as well as creating a distinctive and unusual surface. Together with a group of friends, including the client, Fujimori charred 400 eight-metre boards by hand for the exterior in a single day. The heat of the production process causes the boards to warp to a certain degree. The gaps between them are filled with plaster creating a striking black and white striped effect. The roof is clad in hand-rolled copper shingles. Although the copper was originally an industrially generated product, rolling the shingle elements by hand "killed the industrial commonness" and allows them to harmonise with the other natural materials used for the building. The internal walls are clad in chestnut boards and plaster. The fireplace in the main room is plastered and embedded with pieces of charcoal.

Together with Akira Koyama, Fujimori also landscaped the large, 1825-square-metre surrounding garden, planting it and adding a small hut-like building that serves as a place to rest. The walkways were paved in cement and finished with a hand-brushed texture. The old well on site was restored and the fresh spring water from it redirected through a bamboo conduit. ▶

ENERGY CONCEPT

Since the third century BC, wood has been the building material of choice in Japan. Although in recent years there has been an increase in the use of other materials, such as concrete and steel, wooden structures, particularly for housing, remain the most commonly used in architecture.

Why then, asks Fujimori, has not wood stock been depleted during the past 1800 years as is the case with other countries? The answer, he believes, is the practice of sustainable forestry. A 300-year cyclical system of planting and thinning every 20, 40, 60, 100 and 200 years is traditional in Japan, where by the 300th year the forest is harvested and new trees planted. As an island nation, relatively stable political conditions have helped contribute to the continual success of this cycle of sustainability.

However, sustainability has been dramatically affected in recent years. While a large number of forests were stripped bare during the Second World War and consequently replanted, elevated labour costs have precluded the thinning of these new forests in their 40th and 60th years, preventing trees from growing due to overcrowded conditions. Unfortunately, this has inevitably resulted in a marked deterioration of the forests, especially those of the Japanse cedar. Therefore, to contribute to the sustainability of wooden resources and to open up new possibilities for expression in wooden buildings, Fujimori has chosen to use Japanese cedar in great quantities for the structure and finishing of this residence, with added emphasis on the external wall, in which durability has been increased by carbonisation of the surface of the Japanese cedar. In addition, it has been given a new expression by the interlaminating of plaster and carbonised Japanese cedar. "It is not largely-recognised," says Fujimori, "that wood is the only building material which people can grow and increase its absolute quantity. As long as good forestry management is applied, I believe that wood is the most sustainable building material." ▶

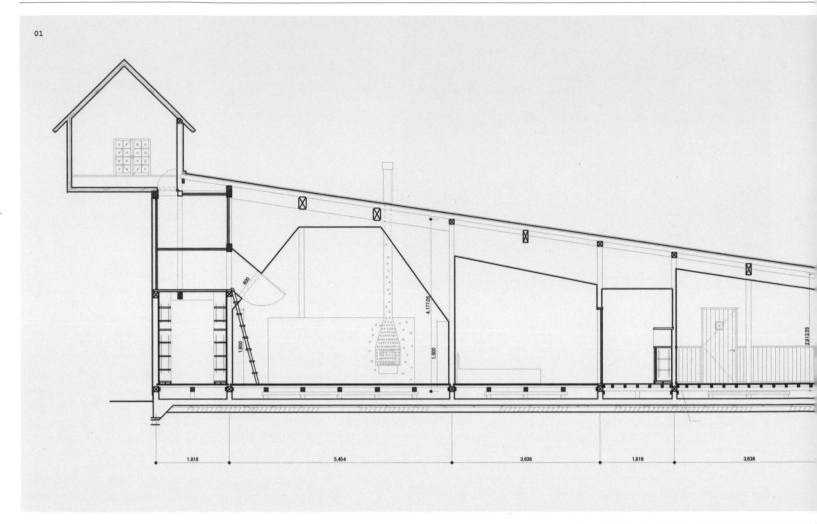

03

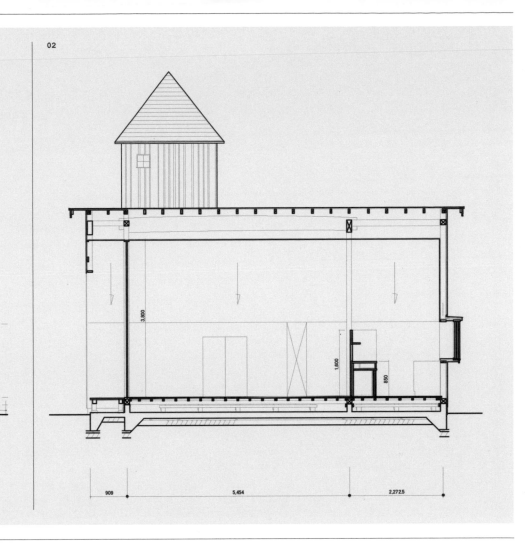

02

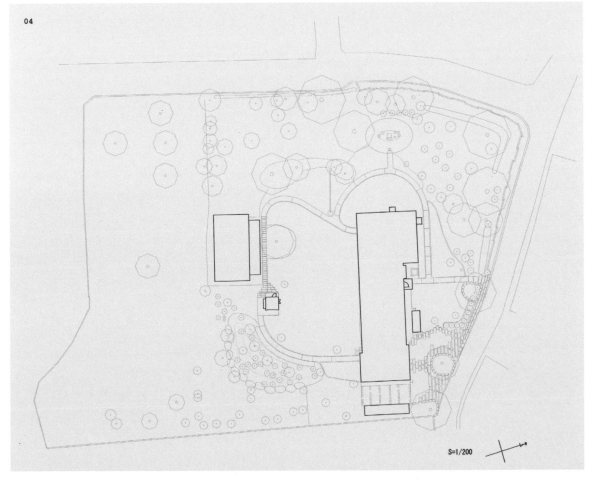

04

01 Longitudinal section.

02 Cross section.

03 A mini tower is perched
on the edge of the build-
ing's highest point.

04 Site plan.

S=1/200

01 Side view. The building appears to be emerging from the sand dunes of the desert.

02/03 Views of entrance situation.

HENDERSON COMMUNITY BUILDING
PATEL ARCHITECTURE INC.: NARENDRA PATEL + ALLAN LECLAIRE

ENGINEER
Knapp & Associates

CLIENT
City of Palm Desert, California

PROJECT LOCATION
Palm Desert, California, USA

COMPLETION DATE
2009

ASSIGNMENT

Beautifully situated with mountain-facing views, the Henderson Community Building (HCB) is designed to form an important centrepiece for the city of Palm Desert and present an image of modern, sophisticated, high-performance green building. It is also intended to rejuvenate the new city park along Highway 111, yet have respect, harmony and communication with the surrounding mountains and desert landscape. ◣

LOCATION

Highly arid desert location with strong sun conditions in an undulating landscape of mountains, rocks and sand dunes. ◣

CONCEPT

The architecture of the HCB is not intended to follow a particular style; rather it has emerged through a specific team-based process. This includes sensibility to social responsiveness, energy use, functionality and ecological awareness. During the initial design process the architects attempt a foreword thinking exercise in climatic control that would allow the building to make use of, rather than ignore, the powerful desert sun. "Anyone can build using lots of material," says Patel. "Taking weight away from things, however, teaches you to make the shape of structures do the works, to understand the limits of strength of components and to replace rigidity with flexibility." Massive walls are combined with light-weight fabric structures juxtaposed between contrasting elements - yet remaining loyal to the maxims "truth to materials" and "honesty of expression". Traditional and new forms of construction are combined in unconventional ways. ◣

REALISATION

The geometry of the HCB is straightforward, based on a dynamic geometry that maximises repetition in most areas of the chamber-of-commerce part of the building. The shape of the western side, with its sweeping curve, produces interactive spaces for community activities. The extensions of the façades beyond the enclosure of the lobby are called "fins" and "perforated screen". Trimmed like a sail on a yacht, the fins serve to lessen the effects of wind, sun and rain on the façade, but most importantly they add a transparent layer to a concrete building.
The concrete, steel and glass with spider fittings assemblage over the main entry are used to provide an external social/public space and to harmonise the space between the lobby and the area outside of the entry. To extend the effect of transparency over the full day/night cycle, the lobby lighting is designed with strong up-lights, making the lobby ceiling inside and the suspended perforated steel canopy outside appear as one and enhancing the sense of arrival. The curving entry lobby grows out of a massive concrete base. The choice of material, colour and texture was important for the architects as it creates a human, earthy feel to the building on all sides. Earth berms echoing the surrounding desert park-forms create a relationship between natural desert landscape and the new building so that the building appears to be emerging from the sand dunes. ◣

ENERGY CONCEPT

The design of the Henderson Community Building provides for a large array of photovoltaic panels on the roof. The entire building shell, including the interior walls, is built from highly insulated panels, covered with high-strength concrete. All wall surfaces and the majority of the ceiling surfaces are kept as a natural concrete finish, which required no paint and no drywall. All floor surfaces are polished concrete, requiring no additional finish material to cover the structural concrete. All material had a high percentage of recycled content, and all waste was carefully managed and sent to recycling facilities. The building process and use of material greatly reduced CO_2 emissions and used fewer natural resources. The focus of green design is, for the project, an opportunity to work in harmony with the natural features and resources surrounding the site, and to use materials that are sustainably grown or recycled rather than new materials from non-renewable resources. All casework was designed with bamboo facing. Paint made without volatile organic compounds and cabinets made without toxins, such as formaldehyde, were specified, with natural stone for counters and flooring being recommended. The project was built without dangerous chemicals. The products and materials specified were chosen because many are manufactured using sustainable manufacturing practices to ensure the most efficient, clean and healthy environment. The architects' commitment to waste management goes beyond safe disposal of hazardous waste. They instruct their contractors to send all plastics, steel, concrete, cardboard, metal, drywall, glass, and more to recycling waste facilities, thus reducing the amount of waste diverted to landfills.
Plumbing fixtures with water conserving features are specified. All landscaping around the building was selected to be desert plants and trees, which require a minimum amount of water. A drip-system irrigation was designed to be even more efficient in water use. Photovoltaic panels were placed in such a way as to generate 20 per cent of the building's electricity needs and run all the computers and some lights in case of power cuts or emergencies. ◣

01 All walls are kept as a natural concrete finish which required no paint and no drywall.

02/03 Elevations of the building.

04 Entrance situation

05 The concrete, steel and glass with spider fittings assemblage over the main entry.

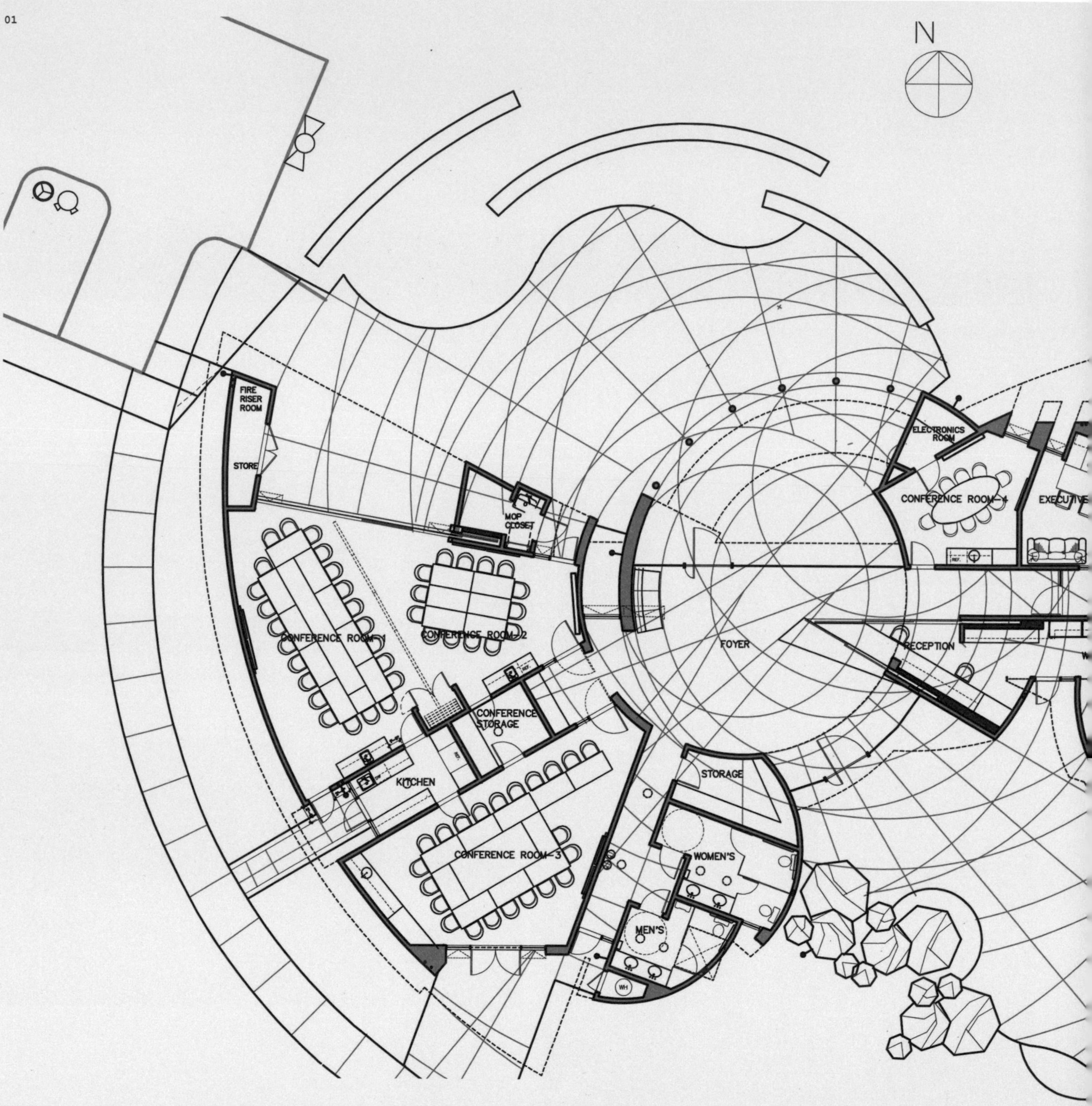

N

FIRE
RISER
ROOM

STORE

MOP
CLOSET

CONFERENCE ROOM-1

CONFERENCE ROOM-2

ELECTRONICS
ROOM

CONFERENCE ROOM-4

EXECUTIVE

FOYER

RECEPTION

CONFERENCE
STORAGE

KITCHEN

STORAGE

CONFERENCE ROOM-3

WOMEN'S

MEN'S

WH

02

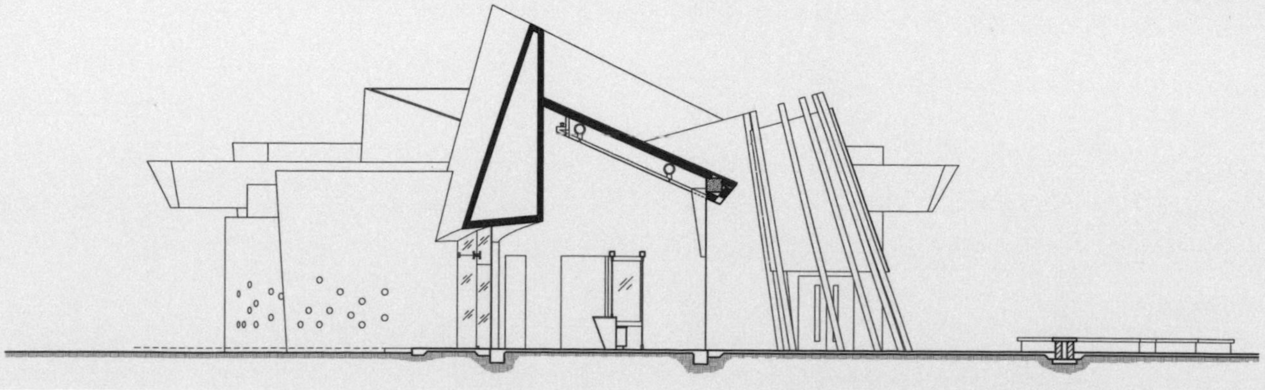

01 Floor plan of
the building

02 Cross section.

111

CHAPTER
02

CROSS COUNTRY

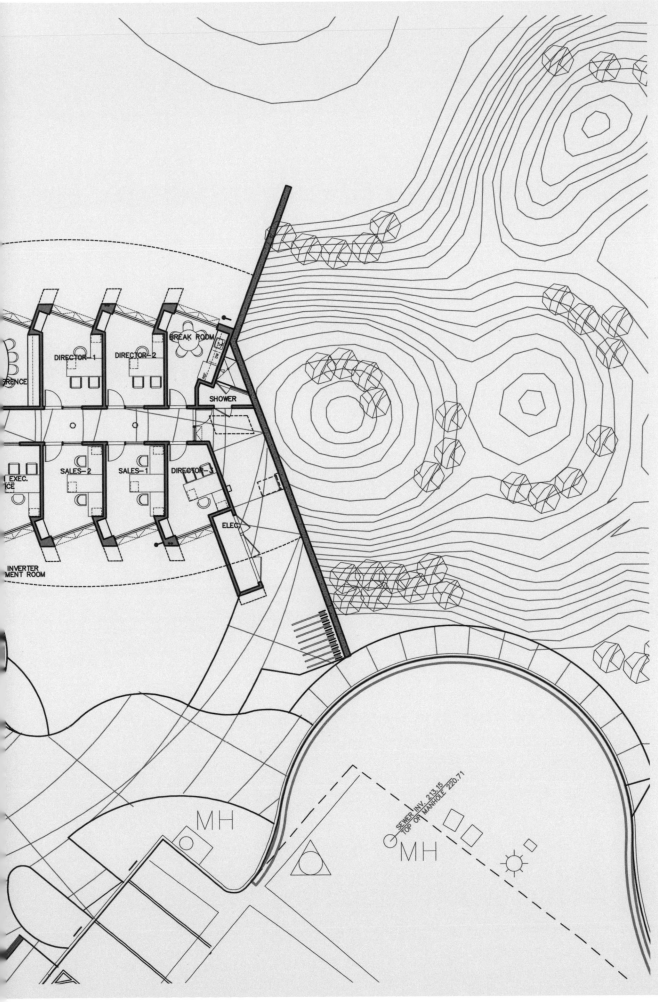

01 The building is constructed on
    pillars on top of a rock ridge.

PRINCESS ELISABETH ANTARCTICA STATION

INTERNATIONAL POLAR FOUNDATION

PROJECT DIRECTOR / CHIEF ENGINEER OF SITE CONSTRUCTION
Alain Hubert

PROJECT COORDINATOR
Johan Berte

PROGRAMME ADMINISTRATOR
Nighat Amin

PROJECT LOCATION
Utsteinen Nunatak, Dronning Maud
Land (East Antarctica)

CLIENT
Belgian Federal
Government

COMPLETION DATE
2009

ASSIGNMENT

The International Polar Foundation (IPF) was set up in 2002 as a public utility foundation with the primary aim of promoting polar research, in particular as a means of understanding the fundamental mechanisms contributing to climate change. The IPF initiates demonstration projects to show how contemporary energy challenges can be surmounted by human ingenuity. This led to the idea of providing a unique platform for international polar research activities during the International Polar Year 2007-2008. It is within this context that the project to build the first "zero emission" station in Antarctica was conceived. The Princess Elisabeth Station will provide the necessary services and facilities to efficiently support international scientific research in the Sør Rondane area in East Antarctica. Subject to extreme conditions, and faced with monumental logistical challenges related to transporting building materials to the Antarctic interior, the station was conceived to achieve high standards for functionality, safety and minimum environmental impact. ◣

LOCATION

The station site, 71°57′ south and 23°20′ east, on the Utsteinen Ridge, north of the Utsteinen Nunatak, Dronning Maud Land, East Antarctica, although ideal in many ways, held certain difficulties, such as the granite geology and powerful katabatic winds.

CONCEPT

Given the high costs to ship fuel all the way to remote Antarctica, the decision was made early to supply the station's energy needs solely with renewable energy sources. From there, it was decided the station would be the first zero emission research station ever, a choice which was backed with ideological considerations in favour of developing sustainable solutions to face the climate challenge. "The most interesting concept of this new structure," says Nighat Amin, "lies in the innovative way in which known building technologies, renewable energy and water treatment technologies have been integrated into a structure and an operating system that is reminiscent of a living organism." It was also a general concern to make this a year-round operating research station, which meant the station would have to be equipped with laboratories and scientific platforms outside the station, designed to hold up to the fiercest winter storms. ◣

The station is located at an altitude of 1400 metres above sea level, is 190 kilometres away from the coast with air temperatures ranging from -5 degrees to -50 degrees Celsius and strong winds gusting up to 250 kilometres per hour. The station was developed according to the laws of aerodynamics, taking into account wind-induced forces, the effects of snow accumulation and snow erosion. It was built on pillars on top of a rock ridge so as to allow the snow to flow under the station, preventing accumulation against the walls of the station and erosion. The station also had to be located close to a source of snow so as to allow for a fresh water supply. ◣

REALISATION

To achieve a compact and energy efficient station, the designers of the new station first studied the characteristics of existing Antarctic buildings extensively to establish a list of guidelines and important lessons learned over the years. But the key components in designing the low-emission station were the user scenarios, since these provided the designers with an accurate view on how people would live in and around the station.

The station was not conceived as a traditional architectural project, but with a method similar to the ones used in systems engineering for space, which puts an emphasis on striking a balance between human requirements and technical limitations rather than on aesthetic considerations.

Another key concept in the station's development lies in its "hybrid design" typology: the living and working quarters are built on pillars, whereas the storage rooms are located in a snow cave beneath the surface.

The main building was designed with a concentric architecture, consisting of various layers built around the technical core room, which holds the water treatment systems, the ventilation system, the station control systems and the batteries for energy storage.

Around this core are three concentric layers: a first one containing the station's active systems such as the kitchen and laundry, a second one including the so-called passive areas such as the living and sleeping rooms, and a third one made up of the insulated outer skin of the station.

The conception, as well as the building and the financing, were carried out by the IPF. The funds raised came from both private sponsors and public partners, i.e. the Belgian Federal Government. All in all, for the construction of the station only, 160 containers, 130 people and 34 weeks of expedition were needed. ◣

01 The main building was designed with a concentric architecture, consisting in various layers built around the technical core room.

02 View of the solar thermal panels and the station.

03 View of the technical core room.

ENERGY CONCEPT

In operation, the station was designed to rely on 100 per cent renewable energies, release zero carbon emissions into the atmosphere and recycle 100 per cent of its waste water. A combination of wind turbines and photovoltaic panels supply the station's electricity during the summer, whereas during the winter the station relies solely on the nine wind turbines. Solar thermal panels provide the station with warm water and melt the snow to provide drinking water for the researchers. Solid wastes, on the other hand, are filled into containers, loaded onto a ship every two years and removed from the Antarctic continent. No waste material remains on site. Finally, the wood and stainless steel structure, along with the various elements of the station were designed with the idea of being easily dismountable. The station can thus, at the end of its mission, be entirely dismantled and shipped back to Belgium. The station's thermal insulation allows minimal heat loss through the station's walls. Each of the 160 side panels composing the walls of the station are made up of nine consecutive layers. The insulation layer itself, lightweight

expanded polystyrene, is 40 centimetres thick. By creating an airtight building, stale air would normally not be able to escape. A sophisticated ventilation system is therefore needed to maintain adequate inside air quality levels. The station is heated by what is known as passive solar gain, a technique optimised by the building's layout and window arrangement. Passive solar gain, combined with the heat released by the core systems and human occupation and regulated by the station's ventilation system, has proved to be so efficient that no other heating system is needed to heat the station during the summer months. All station systems are integrated and piloted by an intelligent central unit. A specifically designed smart grid has been installed inside the Princess Elisabeth Station to manage the energy consumers in balance with the station's energy production by means of intelligent prioritising. Whereas a conventional mini-grid can feed three times more installed consumers than the average energy production can support, the smart grid used at the Princess Elisabeth Station takes

this one step further: it is able to work ten times more installed consumers than the station's average energy production. By means of this energy management system, the electricity generated by the solar panels and wind turbines is distributed directly to appliances through the electrical grid. Any excess energy is stored in batteries located inside the central core of the station. This configuration ensures that working and living conditions inside the station are optimised with minimal resource consumption. This centralised control of interdependent systems also allows for remote monitoring during the winter. In line with the requirements of the Antarctic Treaty to minimise environmental impact, the Princess Elisabeth Station will also be equipped with a specially designed water treatment unit. Inspired by technology developed for the space sector, the two bioreactors and two filtration units will allow the station to treat 100 per cent of its grey and black waters. Most of the recycled water, although fit for human consumption, will be reused for other functions (showers, toilets and washing machines). ◣

01

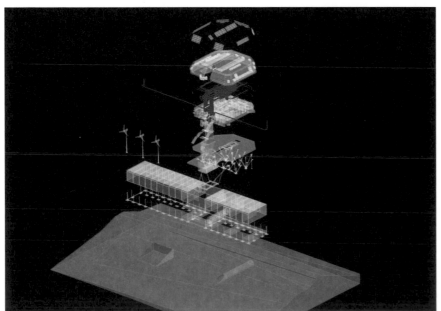

03

02

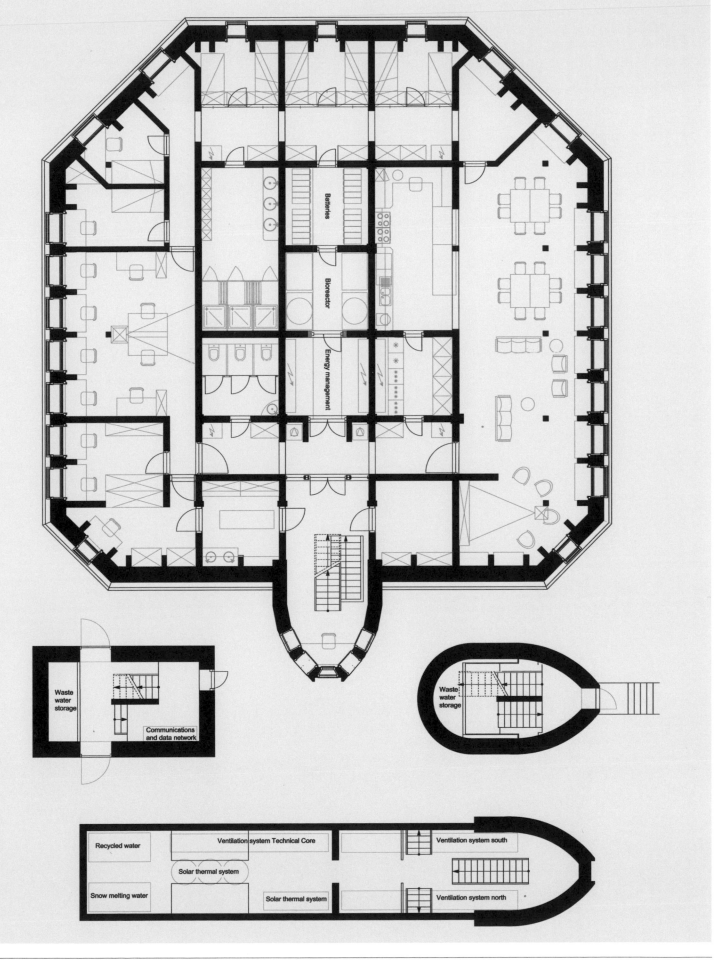

Batteries

Bioreactor

Energy management

Waste
water
storage

Communications
and data network

Waste
water
storage

Recycled water

Ventilation system Technical Core

Ventilation system south

Solar thermal system

Snow melting water

Solar thermal system

Ventilation system north

01 View of the station from above. **02** Isometric view. **03** View of wind turbines that supply the station's electricity. **04** Floor plans of the building.

CLAY FIELD
RICHES HAWLEY MIKHAIL ARCHITECTS

ENGINEER	CLIENT	PROJECT LOCATION	COMPLETION DATE
Buro Happold	Orwell Housing Association	Elmswell, Suffolk, United Kingdom	2008

01 Longitudinal view.
The project provides
the framework for a
sustainable community
across a rural site.

LOCATION

The chosen location was a 1.1-hectare site on the outskirts of the village of Elmswell in rural Suffolk. This East Anglian county in the southeast of England is famous for its gentle rolling countryside, agricultural landscape and pretty medieval villages with black and white half-timbered houses. ◢

CONCEPT

In an area where commuters are pushing house prices beyond the means of local people, in particular young families, Clay Field gives those with a connection to the village of Elmswell the opportunity for an affordable home of their own. The project provides the framework for a truly sustainable community, with a mixture of communal and private spaces alternated with beautiful homes across a rural site. A terrace consisting of three houses forms the basic building block of the scheme. The front façades are clad in continuous cedar weatherboards and shingles with gables in traditional lime render. Variety is brought to the elevations through the responsive positioning and size of windows, arranged to establish the optimal relationship between solar gain and daylight as well as to make the most of views. The low profile and varying scales of the buildings are designed to minimise overshadowing, enabling the low winter sun (typical of the area's flat landscape) to reach all properties. The terraces have been carefully positioned in distinctive groups staggered around public open space. A rural landscaping of swales and dips drains the site, recalling ancient field patterns and promoting diversity of habitat. Public space is seen as a part of larger village life. The three low-maintenance communal gardens, including a wildflower meadow, allotments and an orchard of Suffolk apples, give spaces to cultivate, but also to relax, socialise and allow access for the wider community. The scheme is home to a large number of young families, and children's safety and play were an important aspect to the site and landscape design. The local school has been involved throughout the project. ◢

ENERGY CONCEPT

Three different concerns led the design of sustainable elements of the scheme: (1) passive techniques (maximising solar gain/minimising overshadowing), (2) sustainable specification, and (3) minimising use of resources over the lifespan of the buildings.
(1) Passive techniques: All houses face south and benefit from passive solar gain even on the shortest day of the year. The position and size of glazing are carefully designed to maximise this effect. A rooflight allows for cooling using the stack effect. The massing of the houses on the site and their section has been

ASSIGNMENT

Clay Field's brief was devised for an RIBA competition. It called for 26 affordable homes, with a mixture of rental and shared ownership. Devised by the Suffolk Preservation Society (part of the Campaign for Rural England) and Orwell Housing Association, the brief's aspirations were for exemplary energy-efficient and sustainable housing. The competition was looking for a scheme which interpreted the distinctiveness of Suffolk in a contemporary way. The scheme would also reflect the needs of people living in a rural environment alongside an architecture that could demonstrate that affordable need not necessarily equate to bland. The project was to be developed in consultation with the local Parish Council as well as the future tenants of the houses. ◢

01

02

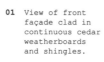

01 View of front façade clad in continuous cedar weatherboards and shingles.

02 Street view.

03 Interior view. Internally, the layout is carefully designed to maximise space, light and through-ventilation.

04 Side view of the buildings facing south.

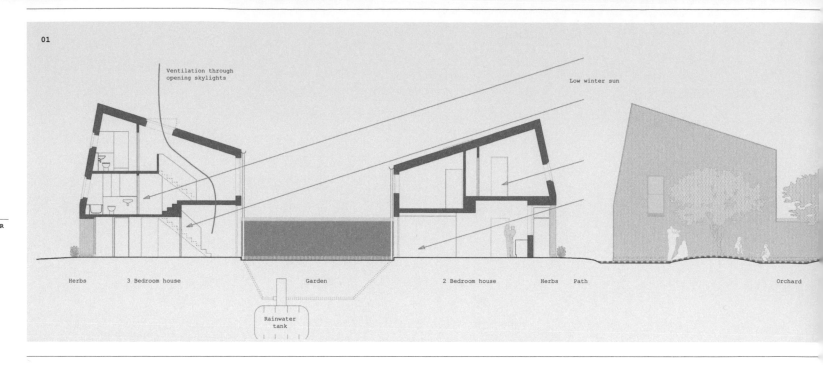

Ventilation through
opening skylights

Low winter sun

Herbs   3 Bedroom house   Garden   2 Bedroom house   Herbs   Path   Orchard

Rainwater
tank

01 Sections illustrating the environmental concept.   **02** Concept diagrams.   **03** Looking across the fence.

designed to minimise overshadowing between properties. (2) Sustainable specification: The project specification strategy was to minimise embodied energy, minimise waste and achieve a highly insulated, airtight, breathable construction, which uses local materials and techniques and minimises maintenance requirements. The key elements involved include: Hempcrete for insulating walls – hemp has the unique ability to lock carbon into the very fabric of the building. This material has excellent environmental and thermal qualities. The use of pre-fabricated timber frames minimised time on site and waste. A calcium silicate board was used as internal cladding; it provides internal finish and gives racking strength to the frame. Forest Stewardship Council-rated cedar was used for all weatherboarding and shingles. All the concrete necessary for foundations used 50 per cent recycled aggregate. A biomass boiler was installed to supply heat and hot water to all houses by burning locally-sourced sustainable fuel. Whole house ventilation system allied with air tight construction) was employed, and the whole construction of each house is breathable for a healthier environment and better performance. A rainwater recycling system was installed with an underground tank and individual header tanks in the houses. This combined with low wateruse fittings in bathrooms and kitchens. Recycled cabinets were installed in the kitchens. (3) Minimising use of resources: The specifications above, alongside the use of passive techniques, minimise the need for heating and water usage within the houses. Thus residents have warm houses and low bills. High levels of daylight reduce requirements for electrical lighting, and the biomass boiler removes any need for gas or electrical heating. Whole house ventilation recovers 80 per cent of heat from internal air, and on-site composting and allotments are provided. ◣

REALISATION

The scheme creates low maintenance, healthy and beautiful family homes with communal gardens, allotments and play spaces to encourage the growth of a strong community. The landscape planting increases biodiversity across the site with a variety of habitats created.
A SUDS system of swales keeps all surface water on site. The project features a number of systems that have helped to make it an energy-efficient build and keep the energy bills low. The project is subject to post-occupancy evaluation by the Sustainability and Alternative Technologies Team at Buro Happold; results to date indicate that the performance of the project is living up to expectations. The houses are constructed of a timber frame, filled with Hempcrete - a sprayed mix of lime and hemp – the first sprayed application in the UK. These Hempcrete walls help to make the construction airtight by embedding the timber-framed structure in the insulation. Garden walls are of unfired clay block protected with lime render. These earthy materials provide a direct visual and perceptual connection to the vernacular architecture of the region. In addition, houses feel solid and built to last. Internally, the layout is carefully designed to maximise space, light and through-ventilation. The floors are staggered with an open stairwell running from the kitchen to the rooflights allowing a through-flow of air, so the homes are ventilated naturally in the summer. In winter, an additional mechanical system removes 80 per cent of heat from outgoing air and uses it to heat incoming air. Alongside the breathable construction of hemp, this ventilation system achieves a truly healthy environment for the families that live here. Other innovations include the use of Isonat - a hemp/linen insulation material, and the use of ground glass blast-furnace slag as a recycled aggregate in concrete foundations. ◣

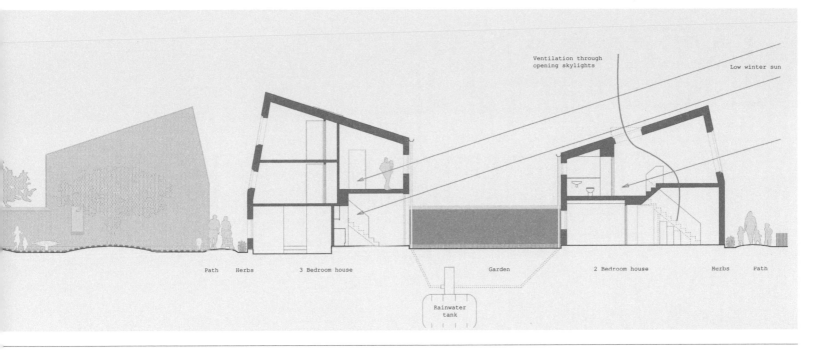

Ventilation through
opening skylights

Low winter sun

Path   Herbs   3 Bedroom house   Garden   2 Bedroom house   Herbs   Path

Rainwater
tank

02

0   50m

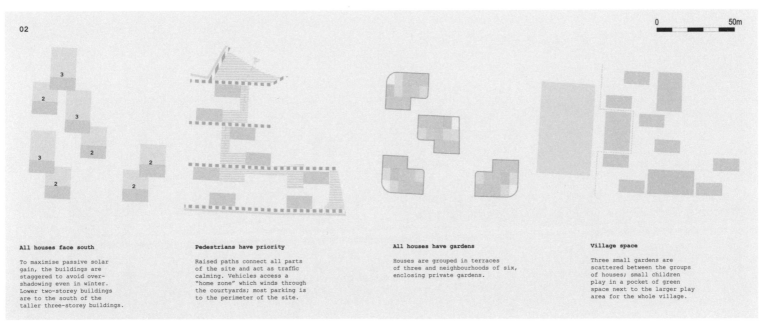

All houses face south

To maximise passive solar
gain, the buildings are
staggered to avoid over-
shadowing even in winter.
Lower two-storey buildings
are to the south of the
taller three-storey buildings.

Pedestrians have priority

Raised paths connect all parts
of the site and act as traffic
calming. Vehicles access a
"home zone" which winds through
the courtyards; most parking is
to the perimeter of the site.

All houses have gardens

Houses are grouped in terraces
of three and neighbourhoods of six,
enclosing private gardens.

Village space

Three small gardens are
scattered between the groups
of houses; small children
play in a pocket of green
space next to the larger play
area for the whole village.

03

MAOSI ECOLOGICAL DEMONSTRATION PRIMARY SCHOOL

EDWARD NG + JUN MU

ENGINEER
Edward Ng, Jun Mu

CLIENT
Kadoorie Farm and Botanic Garden

PROJECT LOCATION
Maosi Village, Xiansheng,
Qingyang City, Gansu Province, China

COMPLETION DATE
2007

01

02

03

04

01/ Impressions of the
02/ Maosi Primary
03 School. The build-
    ings follow the
    topography of the
    landscape.

04 View of spaces for
    concentration and
    contemplation in
    the school's court-
    yard.

05 Children leaving
    school.

06 Aerial view of Maosi
    Primary School.

07 Longitudinal view
    of the classrooms.

05

06

07

01 Cross section.

ASSIGNMENT

Maosi village has around 2500 inhabitants, 200 of whom are schoolchildren. The original, traditional "mud cave" local school was only 3.5 metres by 7 metres in size and held just 20 children. It was far from adequate. The local government built a concrete frame brick school a few years ago that looked modern and cheerful. But it turned out to be too hot in the summer and too cold in the winter. Cow dung and coal needed to be burnt in the winter to keep the classroom warm, which was not only far too expensive for the community but potentially dangerous: eleven students in a similar nearby school were killed by carbon monoxide poisoning recently, say the architects. The local government asked Edward Ng and Jun Mu to produce an ecological school design that would replace four existing schools in the area, providing twelve classrooms for 450 students and twelve offices for teachers as well as facilities such as restrooms and a playground. ◣

LOCATION

The Loess Plateau in China covers an area a few times the size of Germany. It has a population of around 100 million, mostly farmers. The continental climatic conditions in the region are very extreme, ranging from minus 10 to 20 degrees Celsius in the winter to 35 to 40 degrees Celsius in the summer. There is plenty of sunlight but little rain. Maosi village has been inhabited for thousands of years. It is remote and was until recently only accessible via a mud track. The economy is poor and suffers from pollution and soil erosion. Regional education is also in great need of improvement. The Maosi school was designed and constructed to follow the topography of the landscape and be inspired by local traditional houses. Mud cave-like dwellings are the traditional local building style. The high thermal mass of these buildings provides comfortable living spaces, but their size is restricted because of their limited structural strength. ◣

CONCEPT

Together with their client-donor, Ng and Mu aspired to 'build an eco-school that respects local culture, uses local materials and know-how, but improves it with scientific understanding; a school that is cheap and affordable, and provides a better learning environment for the village children'. They also hope that the Maosi school will serve as a prototype, for future schools in the area, that addresses the environmental, social and economic dimensions of sustainability. The architects used a modular approach for ease of construction. Materials were mostly local such as straw, mud and stones gathered from the nearby river. Timber was bought one piece at a time from villagers and second-hand tiles were collected from villagers with disused sheds. ◣

ENERGY CONCEPT

Ng and Mu used locally available natural resources and recycled materials with a minimum amount of embedded energy so as not to impact the local economy. Waste was minimised during construction: rafter off-cuts were re-used for children's facilities, and spare mud bricks were mixed with straw mud for plastering. Compared to conventional local schools, the eco-school has a far better ecological performance in terms of energy consumption and environmental impact. When occupied, the classrooms achieve an acceptable level of thermal comfort without consuming fuel for heating in the winter. According to field measurements in 2007-2008, the indoor air temperature of new classrooms is always stable – cool in summer and warm in winter. Even at unusually cold temperatures in winter, the indoor ambience still had an acceptable thermal comfort with fresh air, without needing coal for heating. Aside from lighting at nighttime, the school consumes little or no total energy annually. This means the limited funds can be spent on learning aids rather than energy. Because the villagers carried out the construction themselves, primarily by hand and with simple tools, the transference of skills during building meant that villagers are now able to improve and maintain the school in the future. ◣

REALISATION

This region was the cradle of Chinese civilisation over 5000 years ago. The village's rich cultural heritage and traditions need to be respected, and the project aimed to do so by creating a humble and appropriate design to achieve a harmonious relationship with both nature and the socio-cultural context of the village. The architects used locally available natural resources and recycled material, including mud bricks, rubble, straw and reed. The school used a traditional local wood beam and column structure, and the villagers themselves were employed to carry out the construction, which enhanced a sense of belonging and communal ownership. The initial ten classrooms were planned in five units at two levels to allow maximum exposure to the south. Using parametric computer simulation software, design options were studied and the best performance/cost option selected. A large thermal mass of mud-brick walls, an insulated traditional roof, and double-glazed windows were incorporated. The semi-buried forms at the north side, together with the direct-gain mode of passive solar system further improved the thermal performance. Angled window openings maximised daylight to the indoor space. As a result, say the architects, the Maosi eco-school costs no more to build than an ordinary, but inappropriate, concrete-brick school. Construction of the school building itself took three months between April and July 2007. ◣

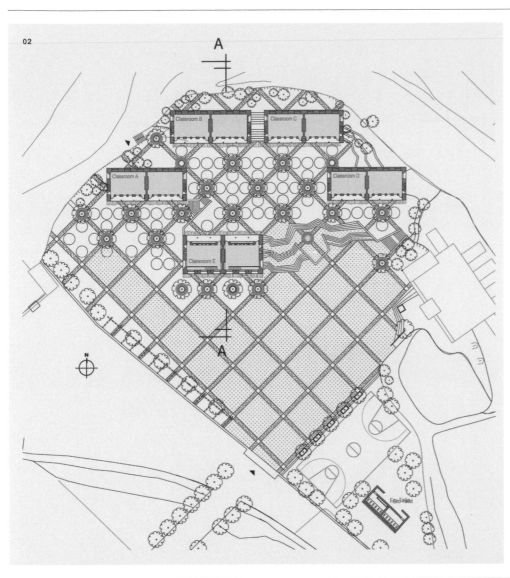

A

A

Classroom B Classroom C

Classroom A Classroom D

Classroom E

02 Site plan.

03 / South elevation
04 of the classroom.

05 Construction process.

06 The school is inspired
by the local building
style, such as the
traditional mud caves
of this region.

ENGINEER
Ryota Kidokoro, Yoshiyuki Mori (Arup Japan)

CLIENT
Soichiro Fukutake

PROJECT LOCATION
Inujima, Okayama, Japan

COMPLETION DATE
2008

INUJIMA ART PROJECT
HIROSHI SAMBUICHI ARCHITECTS

01 The task for the architects was to create
   a completely natural
   energy-driven air-
   conditioned museum
   which consumes no fossil
   energy resources what-
   soever.

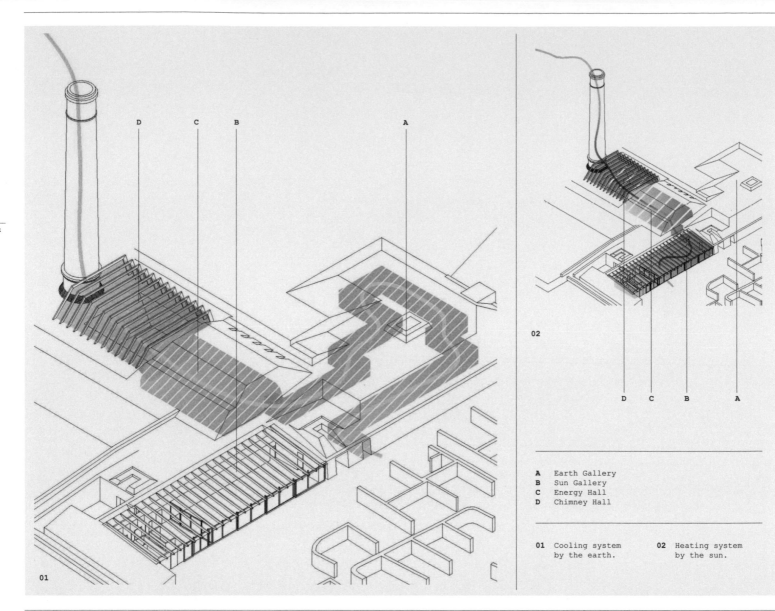

A Earth Gallery
B Sun Gallery
C Energy Hall
D Chimney Hall

01 Cooling system by the earth.

02 Heating system by the sun.

03 Inujima is an isolated island in the Seto Inland Sea in Japan.

ASSIGNMENT

Inujima island in Japan once housed a copper refinery. After a century of disuse, the property was purchased by the wealthy businessman Soichiro Fukutake, who wanted to rehabilitate the site and build a museum that would have minimal impact on the environment. He commissioned the architect Hiroshi Sambuichi to design the new complex and the conceptual artist Yukinori Yanagi to design the permanent installations. The task for the architects was to create a completely natural energy-driven, air-conditioned art-appreciation box which consumes no fossil energy resources whatsoever. The client also wanted the ruins to be renovated to create a sophisticated and unprecedented art island run on natural energy. ◤

LOCATION

Inujima is an isolated island in the Seto Inland Sea in Japan. Originally, it flourished as a granite quarry. A copper refinery was constructed on the site in 1909 but was shut down after ten years. Since then it has remained almost untouched for almost 100 years, and all that remained were the ruins, old quarries and refinery plants. ◤

CONCEPT

From the outset, the architect perceived all the existing materials on the island, such as the old architecture of the ruins, the geography, open spaces, the infrastructure of the factories, waste, and so on, as regenerative resources. The new museum, he felt, had to be in complete symbiosis with the environment and itself part of the natural cycle of growth, weathering and decay. The size, capacity and details of the new architecture were planned according to natural reproduction cycles based on energies extracted from reusable existing landforms and ruined construction elements, usable and sustainable natural resources and waste, as well as newly imported materials. The architects' proposal was to control the art museum's environment using only sustainable natural energies: "Our idea is completely different from existing natural high-tech energy applications, such as solar panels or wind power, and even rejects the idea of converting the energy into electricity," says Sambuichi. "This is because we believe that the true meaning of the term 'sustainable environment' can only be realised when the system is used in tandem with perpetual natural activities." ◤

REALISATION

Since almost all of the island consists of granite, Sambuichi decided to use its heat capacity effectively. In selecting and analysing Karami bricks (a by-product of the copper refinery) and slag, which were lying around the shoreline, his team discovered their useful heat characteristics. As a result, they recycled Karami bricks and slag for the construction of the floor and walls as heat storage and heat-conducting materials. Corten steel was chosen as a further main construction element weathered and oxidised to represent the high-iron content of the island geology. Roofs were made of timber – a renewable resource. Sambuichi chose to build within the ruins of the refinery between the tallest of the five distinctive, yet defunct, smokestacks and the remains of the brick factory structure that spread out towards the sea. Although the chimney stacks were no longer suitable for their function, they still had a chimney effect whereby air is sucked in at the bottom and blown out of the top. The architect took advantage of the presence of one of the chimneys and adapted it as part of an interesting environmental control mechanism for the building to modulate internal temperature: the chill from underground cools the air of one gallery (Earth Gallery), the sun warms another gallery called the Sun Gallery, and in a third power hall, the Chimney Hall, the sun's energy combines with the updraft from the chimney as a third source. The three heat levels are mixed together and controlled in a fourth space, the Energy Hall. Visitors approach the gallery from across the sea, heading towards the distinctive smokestack. When they arrive, they follow a weathered Corten steel wall to an opening in the granite exterior of the building. An 80-metre, steel-clad corridor leads underground into the Earth Gallery, which is illuminated by a single skylight and a collection of mirrors. The Sun Gallery and Chimney Hall at the base of the smokestack are drenched in bright sunlight which filters across in soft, diffuse light to the Energy Hall. The four spaces comprise the main complex, which, along with vegetation and the water-cycling landscape, make up the overall facility. ◤

ENERGY CONCEPT

The Earth Gallery has a base of rough iron for the structural material, which also has a large heat capacity. Iron sheets were bent into waves for structural strength and to expand surface area. The twisting corridor plan encourages air movement. Natural light enters through a north-facing skylight; mirrors mounted at the corners bring sunlight into the rest of the interior by reflection. When walking up the gallery towards the sky, visitors can feel cooling air and the effect of earth heat. In the Sun Gallery, Karami bricks are used as flooring materials, which can store heat from sunlight. Glass is used as the roof material to collect heat. Visitors passing through experience the power of the free energy of solar radiation. The Energy Hall has the same temperature and humidity throughout the year. Its stable atmosphere is maintained by opening and closing windows and doorways to the Earth and Sun Galleries. The interior finish here is cedarwood, which has a low heat capacity and thus absorbs minimal heat into the surface of the walls.

In contrast, Inujima granite, with its large heat capacity, was used for the flooring to allow visitors to feel its warmth and also because it is beautiful and of high-quality, says the architect. Above ground, the air continues along the natural convection path, circulating by changing its density following the sunlight. The Chimney Hall is the engine used to circulate the air. The art placed here is kinetic, allowing visitors to experience the mechanism of the natural convection visually and understand how the chimney works. Traditional buildings such as art museums increase in energy consumption in step with the number of visitors; this places a greater burden on the environment, resulting in humanity having a negative influence on the planet. Sewage from the museum toilets is converted into fertiliser for the island's plants. In other words, the plants outside the buildings will flourish as the number of visitors increases. This brings stability to the microclimate and gives natural beauty and comfort to the site and benefits humanity. Making humans part of the original environmental cycle along with animals, plants, sun, earth, water and air, say the architects, is part of a realistic and sustainable long-term view. ◤

01 Looking down on the landscaped site.

02 The earth gallery buried
into the earth.

03 Remains of the brick factory structure.

04 View of Inujima island from
the water side.

01

02

03

04

07

06

05 Conceptual artist
Yukinori Yanagi
was commissioned to
design permanent
installations.

06 The installation
connects with the
site's materiality.

07 View of gallery.

LA VALL D'EN JOAN
BATLLE I ROIG ARQUITECTES

01

PROJECT LOCATION

COMPLETION DATE

Parc del Garraf, Spain

2008

03

01   The former dump site.

02   Downhill view of pathway. A system of hills and banks avoids water erosion.

03   All building elements have a strong sculptural character.

04   Uphill view of pathway.

05   Areal view. The scheme operates by carrying fluids contained by rubbish through a cleansing process.

06/   Housed in large steel
07   cages, some of the rubbish has remained above ground as a permanent reminder of the site's previous life.

ASSIGNMENT

La Vall d'en Joan (The Valley of Joan) project, designed by Spanish architects Batlle i Roig, has transformed a 600,000 by 200,000 square metre dump site into a green terraced agricultural landscape. ▶

CONCEPT

The project is a striking redrawing of a previously scarred and polluted landscape. The general idea behind the initiative was to create a system of hills and banks in a manner that would avoid water erosion and restore the rubbish dump to nature with a natural design. In this way, the waste deposit restoration project also seeks to return the area to public use. The proximity to urban areas, access and parking facilities give it accessibility and the character of a new entrance to Parc del Garraf. ▶

LOCATION

The landscape restoration project of the controlled dumpsite is located in Parc del Garraf within the municipal borders of Begues and Gavà, both in the Baix Llobregat region. The landfill has been servicing Barcelona's metropolitan area for over 30 years. More than 20 million tons of rubbish were deposited in the valley before the site was closed in 2006. In some places, one would have to dig hundreds of metres before reaching soil. ▶

REALISATION

Work to transform the site – the largest landfill in Spain – began in 2000 and was completed in 2008. The restoration project defines a pattern of topographic configuration, with terraces, side slopes, a drainage system of internal fluids (separated from the external drainage net), a bio gas extraction net, pathways and plantation by phases. Some of the rubbish has remained above ground. Housed in large steel cages which flank the entrance to the site, they serve as a permanent reminder to visitors of the site's previous life. ▶

ENERGY CONCEPT

An on-site underground drainage system filters contaminated waste fluids. Part of this recycled water is then used to irrigate the park. Furthermore, the dump uses emitted biogas to provide electricity. The goal of the entire restoration project is that Parc del Garraf will absorb the dump using local forest matter and support the establishment of primary ecosystems and their development and succession which, over time, will transform the site environment. The site is planted with hearty local species that require little water and are adapted to the local environment. The landscaping is planned with local varieties of shrubs (such as Bardissa, Brolla or Mediterranean Maquis) and trees. ▶

THE HIGH LINE
JAMES CORNER FIELD OPERATIONS
WITH DILLER SCOFIDIO + RENFRO

CONSULTANTS
Diller Scofidio + Renfro (architecture), Buro Happold (Structural/MEP engineering), Robert Silman Associates (structural/historic preservation engineering), Piet Oudolf (horticulture), L'Observatoire International (lighting design)

CLIENT
Public-private partnership between the City of New York (including the following four agencies: NYC Department of Parks & Recreation, Office of the Deputy Mayor for Economic Development, NYC Economic Development Corporation, NYC Department of City Planning) and Friends of the High Line.

PROJECT LOCATION
New York, USA

COMPLETION DATE
Section 1, 2009

01 The design is a redevelopment of an abandoned, elevated freight railway that spans 22 blocks through the west side of Manhattan.

ASSIGNMENT

Field Operations won the 2004 international competition for the design of the High Line, a 1.9-kilometre-long, abandoned elevated railway in New York City. The brief challenged designers to work with the existing structure, to retain elements of the abandoned High Line landscape and artefact, and to give the High Line a compelling new life and future as a one-of-a-kind recreational amenity and grand, public promenade. The design had to be especially innovative and creative in its physicality and dimensions; promotion of green materials and practices; phased implementation, short-and long-term planning; and consideration of future maintenance and operations. ◤

LOCATION

The former railway line runs through the west side of Manhattan. The elevated structure crosses over 22 public streets and weaves in between the dense city fabric, tightly set between buildings and stretching over private property and public streets. ◤

CONCEPT

James Corner's Field Operations design concept evolves from the respect of the innate character of the High Line itself: its singularity and linearity and its emergent properties with wild plant-life – meadows, thickets, vines, mosses, flowers – intermixed with ballast, steel tracks, railings, and concrete. Field Operations' aesthetic and conceptual strategy propose to capitalise on what is already there, to grow something new out of something old. Thereby Field Operations' design solution is primarily threefold: firstly, invention of a new paving system, built from linear concrete planks with open joints, specially tapered edges and seams that permit the free flow of water and the intermingling of organic plant-life with harder materials. Secondly, to slow things down, to promote a sense of duration. Long stairways, meandering pathways, and hidden niches encourage taking one's time. The third approach involves a careful sense of dimension of scale. The result is an episodic and varied sequence of public spaces and landscapes which respond to their context, but are set along a simple and consistent line - a line that cuts across some of the most remarkable elevated vistas of Manhattan and the Hudson River. The design accentuates and elongates transitions, from streetside to topside, hard to soft, woodland to grassland, river to city. Access points are designed as durational experiences of approach and discovery, connecting areas of urban activity below with the High Line above. ◤

REALISATION

As a public-private partnership between the City of New York and the Friends of the High Line, the realisation of the High Line underwent intense community participation in the form of ongoing workshops and presentations, intricate agency coordination with federal, state and city agencies all providing funding to the project, and concentrated private donor engagement to fund specific elements on the line as well as set up an endowment for the maintenance and operation of the park once opened to the public. Opened in spring 2009, the first section of the High Line park spans almost 12,000 square metres and is over 0.8 kilometres long. The striated planking system is designed as a continuous, single surface, yet is built from individual linear precast concrete planks with open joints to encourage emergent growth. At specific locations, planks transform into a ramp or stairway for access to the street level, peel up into seating, or rise into an elevated pathway through a grassland or woodland area. The amount of paving is calibrated to accommodate a variety of uses. All of the planting areas on the High Line are underlined with green-roof or living roof layers including a water retention, drainage and aeration panel, gravel base layer and filter fabric. New plantings build upon the existing landscape character, working with specific environmental conditions and microclimates. A dominant grassland matrix provides consistency, with punctuated and theatrical blooms of perennials, trees and shrubs for diversity, seasonal interest, texture, fragrance, and height and colour variation. The design incorporates most of the existing steel rail tracks. Energy-efficient LED lighting is installed at waist-level and below, illuminating the pathway for safety, while allowing the eye to appreciate the city beyond and the night-time sky. ◤

ENERGY CONCEPT

The High Line as a precedent urban park promotes timely and relevant principles of ecological sustainability, urban regeneration and re-use and conservation over new construction. In total, the High Line reclaims over six acres of former industrial land for new use. The project establishes an urban corridor for habitat, wildlife and people and provides opportunity for future links between greenways and parkways along the Hudson River. In addition to providing valuable open space for the city of New York, the High Line has been estimated by the New York City Deputy Mayor for Economic Development to have already generated $4 billion in private investment in adjacent residential buildings, stores and hotels. In the design process, as much of the original structure as possible was reused, implementing the localised restoration and repair of concrete and steel on an as-needed basis. A new drainage and waterproofing layer was designed and coordinated with the landscape to maximise soil depth and low points in the planting beds, minimising future irrigation requirements. All new plant species have been carefully selected to produce a primarily native, resilient, and low-maintenance landscape. A highly engineered soil specification was developed by soil scientists on the team taking into account urban and elevated extreme conditions, minimal soil depth available and long-term maintenance requirements. The High Line's long-term economic and ecological goals extend well beyond the site's boundaries. It has been a true conduit for urban regeneration and new types of urban open space, contributing to the advancement of ecological and sustainable design. ◤

01 All new plant species have been carefully selected to produce a primarily native, resilient landscape.

02 Northern Spur Preserve, between West 16th Street and West 17th Street, looking south towards the Statue of Liberty.

03 Hard-soft ratio diagrams. The arrangement of tapered planks gradually grade down into planting beds, affording an elongated transition between hard and soft areas.

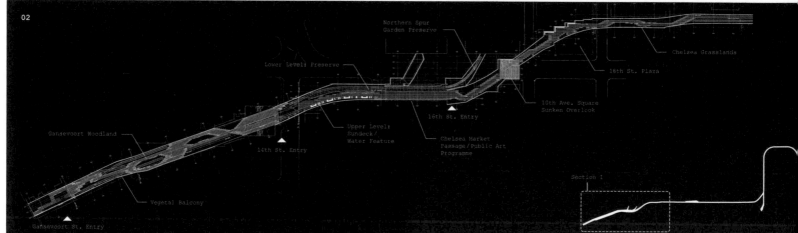

01 Illustration of the former railway
    line that runs through the west side
    of Manhattan.

02 Illustration of completed Section I.

03 View from above. The project es-
    tablishes an urban corridor for
    habitat, wildlife and people.

04 Elevation of Section I.

05 View of parkway with the main seating
    element, a custom designed peel-up
    bench which grows out of the paving.

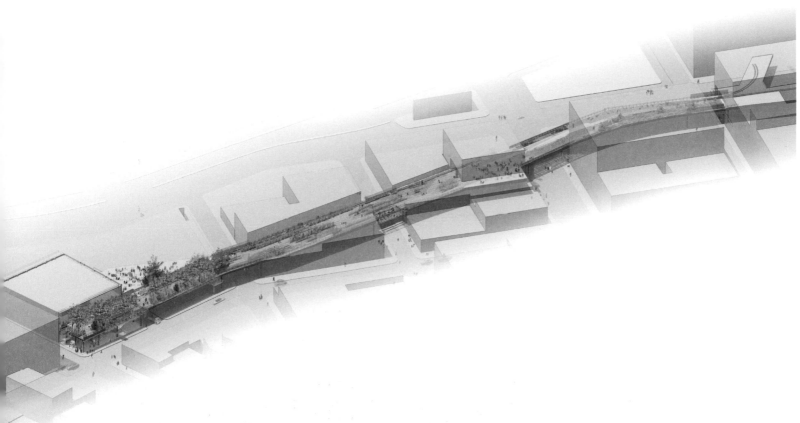

02

01 Entrance at Gansevoort Street and
    Washington Street, looking north.

02 View of slow stair at Gansevoort
    Street.

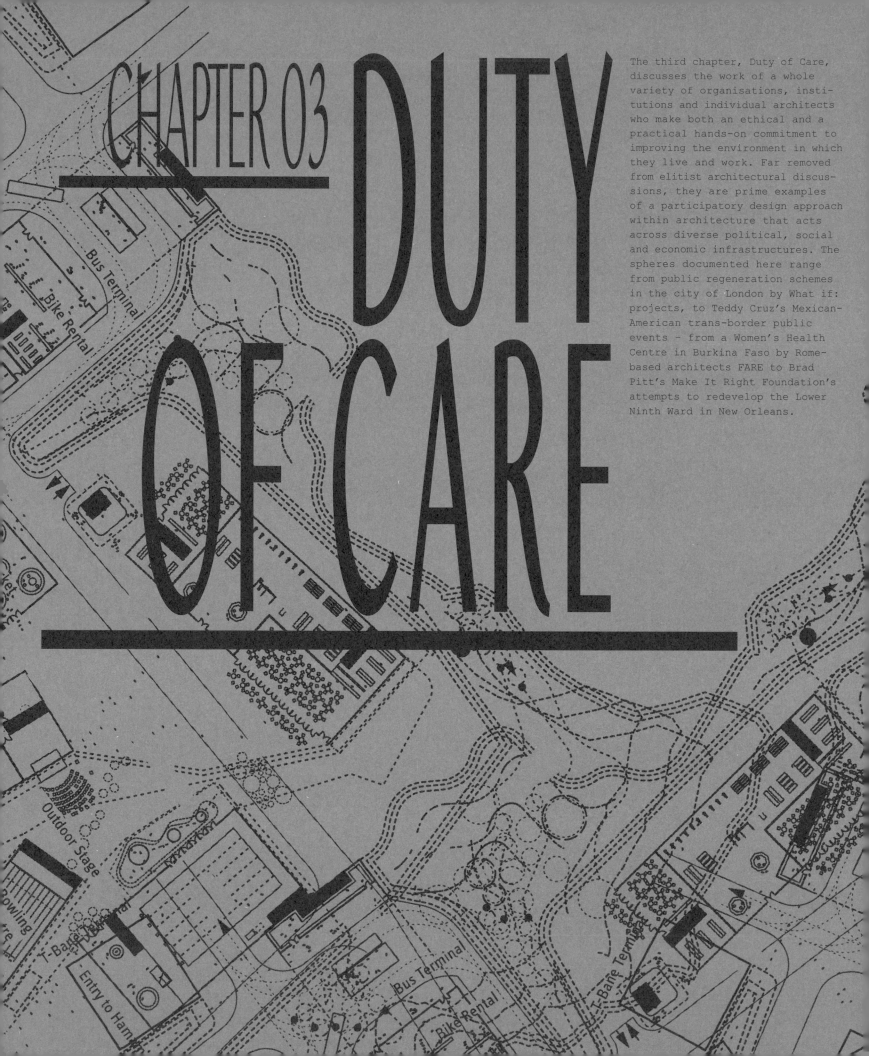

CHAPTER 03 DUTY OF CARE

The third chapter, Duty of Care, discusses the work of a whole variety of organisations, institutions and individual architects who make both an ethical and a practical hands-on commitment to improving the environment in which they live and work. Far removed from elitist architectural discussions, they are prime examples of a participatory design approach within architecture that acts across diverse political, social and economic infrastructures. The spheres documented here range from public regeneration schemes in the city of London by What if: projects, to Teddy Cruz's Mexican-American trans-border public events – from a Women's Health Centre in Burkina Faso by Rome-based architects FARE to Brad Pitt's Make It Right Foundation's attempts to redevelop the Lower Ninth Ward in New Orleans.

LUKAS FEIREISS IN CONVERSATION WITH CHRIS LUEBKEMAN PART I

UNFOLDING TOMORROW / THRIVING FOR FICTIONS OF OUR MULTIPLE FUTURES

Chris Luebkeman is a Director and head of Arup's global Foresight and Innovation Initiative. He explores emerging trends and the impact they might have on the engineering business and its clients. In 2004 he was named a Senior Fellow of the Design Futures Council.

OUR BELIEFS CAN'T BE PROVED BUT THEY ARE SOMETHING WE - AS ANIMALS WITH VERY LARGE BRAINS - HAVE CONSTRUCTED TO HELP US UNDERSTAND THE WORLD AROUND US .

LF: Mr. Luebkeman, you are currently working with some of the world's largest companies and developing scenarios to help them better understand how change creates opportunities in the built environment. How do you picture our future environment, and what new approaches do you envision?

CL: The question is what we imagine and how we imagine it. I believe most of us already have a very good perception, internally as thinking beings, of the challenges which are to come. I believe that humans have three ways in which they process information about today, yesterday and tomorrow. The first is a gut reaction; an animal instinct as Homo sapiens. This is an inexplicable but very deep and real experience that we have as cognisant animals in confrontation with our environment and others. The second reaction is our belief structure. This is when we say: "I believe in this." Our beliefs can't be proved but they are something we - as animals with very large brains - have constructed to help us understand the world around us. We can believe in one god, or two gods, or that every living thing is a god. We can believe that god is a he or a she or whatever. But these are belief structures, which no one can prove. We don't know if they are false or correct. Dolphins and elephants have families too; they also love, hate and communicate. But we don't know whether they believe, as we believe, in certain things, because belief is something essentially human. The third way we process information is through our analytical capability

remember that everything we do evolves around us humans. One doesn't build a hotel as a hospitality experience simply from the bricks, the mortar or the wood. We are trying to provide a place for people. Therefore we focus on people, on human needs and desires as they are today and as we anticipate them in the context of tomorrow. But tomorrow is a story. The future is fiction. It is the story which we tell in order to help us understand what might unfold. Some individuals write a story like a detective novel, others write science fiction or maybe a romance, but all of these stories are fictions. Nobody really knows who and what we are supposed to trust. For us, it is therefore of paramount importance that it is the threefold approach of the gut, the heart and the head that creates the context of the story that will unfold tomorrow. If we are going back to thinking about the hotel, we try to identify the needs and the desires of the persons in that experience today. We are trying to map all of these factors in a process we call life-mapping or experience-mapping. We put together the numerous multi-stake holders in this equation, such as the chef, the banker, the designer, the operator, and the tour guide, and map the kind of experience with which they are confronted today. Then, like the British icon Doctor Who, we pretend that we are all jumping into his time-travel space ship, the TARDIS, to travel through time. We step into the TARDIS and then step out into a new world in 20 years' time. This world then is the one

THE FUTURE IS FICTION. IT IS THE STORY WHICH WE TELL IN ORDER TO HELP US UNDERSTAND WHAT MIGHT UNFOLD.

to take numbers and to project, to cast, to charge them into the future and to use numbers to model what we consider other types of reality. Our method when we are trying to help others think about the future and understand the future is based on touching on all three of these realms. We do this through multiparty workshops. These workshops are based around a singular theme. That theme could be, for example, the hotel of the future. So if we are really looking at the hotel, we have to

in which we picture or paint the new experience map. In order to paint the new experience map, however, we have to picture the new context, the new world, as it is or might be. Here it is very useful to use the heart and the head to ask ourselves what we believe will happen in 20 years' time and what our analysis then begins to tell us about trends. We paint a picture of the context of tomorrow, using variably steep categories, namely social, technological, environmental, economic and political. ▶

This way we make sure that the story we are authoring together about this new context integrates all major aspects and questions that touch on society. How will people interact? What might they be looking at and what might they be reading? What technologies will prevail? How will people be communicating? What technology will be used in 20 years' time? What economic systems will there be? Will it be a new socio-capitalistic-communistic era, a new vision that we don't yet know? Will there still be nation states? Will Europe or the United States still be allies, or will they be divided? The list of questions is endless. The painting of this picture of the world into which we will step is a fascinating process because there's never a singularity. One very important thing for me to remember and to remind others when I am

LF: Taking into consideration that today the whole building industry is facing entirely new challenges and responsibilities that go well beyond one discipline's horizon of experience, it seems to me that if these challenges are to be met, any monocausal approach is doomed to fail and an integrative approach must be taken to break down the boundaries between architecture and city planning and other spheres of knowledge and experience. Now, with your experience in drawing from a vast pool of experts across the world, what is your key to acquiring new insights and being able to see and think out of the box – to connect the gut, the heart and the head as you call it?

CL: At one point, the architect was actually seen as the individual who would unify these three realms. If

THERE WILL NEVER BE ONE FUTURE. THERE WILL BE MULTIPLE FUTURES.

working with them is that there will never be one future. There will be multiple futures. There are certain things like our environment, the air and the sun that are at unity, but the actual physical manifestation of the planet is highly variable. When we are looking at the context of tomorrow, we have to remember that it will be very different depending on where we are on the planet. When we are creating these scenarios, these plausible futures, these stories of tomorrow, the root of this process is the belief in a designed method, a synthetic process of bringing together the right and left side of the brain. This combination is fundamental to understanding

we go back in history and look at architectural writing, we see that they were the most brilliant practitioners and theoreticians before modern times. There was really a combination of the true understanding of a technique and the overall understanding of the human condition and beauty in general which characterised these individuals. I deeply believe that somehow in the last 50 years, architects have lost touch with the fact that we are not making edifices for ourselves, but we are really making places for people, for living and breathing people – and not just to survive as humans, but to thrive as members of a planetary ecosystem and

I BELIEVE VERY STRONGLY IN A MIXTURE OF THE EMOTIVE AND THE ANALYTICAL.

change in robust way. I believe very strongly in a mixture of the emotive and the analytical. I don't believe in trusting only your gut, or in trusting only numbers. Because if you trust only one and not the other, you are missing out on an awful lot that makes us human. ▶

society, of which we are only one member. As an industry, we got very wrapped up in the hierarchical understandings of men at the top of the pyramid and the world for us to master rather than to participate in and work with. I just wrote an essay for the RIBA on the role of

IF THE PROFESSION IS NOT CAREFUL, THE ARCHITECT WILL END UP JUST LIKE THE BLACKSMITH AND BECOME COMPLETELY INSIGNIFICANT TO THE SUCCESSFUL THRIVING OF A SOCIETY.

the architect in 2184. It was a strange, dark essay but the fundamental belief that I have about the role of the architect is quite simple: a profession can become obsolete. There have been professions that have been absolutely vital for the survival of a society. At one time, about two or three thousands years ago, the blacksmith was of greatest importance for a village. If you had a good blacksmith, someone who understood the art and craft of turning stone into metal, your spears were stronger, and you thrived as a village and therefore as a society. The blacksmith was truly the giver of life and death. Now, think of the role of the blacksmith today. We all know of the blacksmith, we might even learn about blacksmiths in school, but the blacksmith today is completely irrelevant to society. No village's or city's success depends on the blacksmith anymore. If the profession is not careful, the architect will end up just like the blacksmith and become completely insignificant to the successful thriving of a society. Instead of being a core contributor to the health and well-being of a community, the architect might very well become the irrelevant blacksmith. I think this extreme example extends to the built environment as a whole. With climate change, with the limits of resources, with energy constraints and with the degradation of the condition of many of our cities around the world, today there's a new awareness in the building industry that we need to be better about understanding the interaction and integration of the systems which allow us to survive and thrive. One of these systems, for example, is one's access to opportunity, which is mobility. Again, this is no longer really a simple question of transportation. For me, the question really is the opportunity an individual has to have a job, how to access it. It could be over the internet, it could be a walk or a drive. The access to opportunity is fundamental. So my plea for our industry is to go back to the fundamentals of our discipline and to reflect on why we are in it. Fundamentally, it is about making places that are healthy and sustainable and that allow individuals to love being in a space. This leads us to another great challenge. Today, we see hundreds and thousands of teenagers playing internet games in which their environments are very rich. Rich in the sense that the experiences these kids are having in the virtual world far exceed the experiences they have in their physical world. It's way too easy just to say that one can do anything on a computer, and it's much more challenging to ask: why is our built environment like this and what can we do now, step by step, little by little, to make it more sustainable for humans? I believe the new challenge for architects and engineers all over the world is to reconsider and revive our built environment as places where we thrive and not simply survive. ▸

I BELIEVE THE NEW CHALLENGE FOR ARCHITECTS AND ENGINEERS ALL OVER THE WORLD IS TO RECONSIDER AND REVIVE OUR BUILT ENVIRONMENT AS PLACES WHERE WE THRIVE AND NOT SIMPLY SURVIVE.

Continuation on page 180.

UNIVERSITY OF TALCA
STUDENTS FROM THE SCHOOL OF ARCHITECTURE

PROJECT LOCATION
Talca, Chile

COMPLETION DATE
Ongoing

01 The Pinohuacho Observation Deck in Chile's
remote countryside. Design by Rodrigo Sheward.

01 Landmark route. One of seven wooden modules
   placed in the landscape, used as info points
   and places to rest. Design by Ronald
   Hernandez, Marcelo Valdes, and Osvaldo Veliz.

02 Box in Canelillo designed by Ingrid Vega.
   The one-unit gallery has a lattice-pattern
   façade with long wood frames in a crossing
   style.

03 Detailed view of façade.

03

02

04 Keepers House designed by Gabriel Vergara.

05 Wood cabins designed by Andres Lillo for cowboys at work in the mountain region.

ASSIGNMENT

Since 2004 the School of Architecture at the University of Talca, Chile, has carried out an On-site Studio and a unique graduation modality that require students to be able to identify a problem whose solution can be addressed through architecture or through the intervention of an architect. Students are then asked to design the solution for that problem, to acquire funds for its implementation, and to direct and supervise its actual construction. This stimulates students to take the initiative, invent and manage their own assignments, and be generally ahead of client expectations. ◣

REALISATION

The works of the School of Architecture at the University of Talca are all conceived to be strongly linked to both visible and invisible conditions of the place to which they belong. They are indeed considered as part of the information that configures the problem or as an assignment for design, management and construction: budget restrictions; the qualification of local workers and the search and development of a sustainable and economic structural solution which introduces innovative ways of using conventional or leftover material. A strong collaborative engagement with future users is a necessary element considered in the process of design and construction. As a result, very different work emerges: some of it emphasises particular tectonics created out of modest materials; other work points to lightness as a value both for sustainability and elegance; other work is innovative in the use of conventional materials, while yet other is a catalyst for social integration, or allows for local culture to adapt and be sustainable over time. In some work, local conditions allow for a new programme to be introduced for users to increase their incomes. ◣

LOCATION

The Chilean region known as the Central Valley, where the School of Architecture is located, is one of the poorest in the country, normally situated at the bottom in national competitive rankings. Nevertheless, it is top ranking in agro-export products and produces high-quality derived products such as wine and fruits. ◣

CONCEPT

Situated in a rural region characterised by a lack of professionals, and whose inhabitants, by consequence, are generally unaware of the work or potential work of an architect, students of the On-site and Graduating Studio engage themselves with local communities and demands. In recent years, more than 100 public buildings have been realised for less privileged social groups by carefully considering territorial and climatic conditions, available materials and local resources. All in all, the programme of education is intended fundamentally to be an engine which, through the search of innovation, transforms knowledge into wealth in an environment that provides plenty of possibilities but is short on economic resources. ◣

ENERGY CONCEPT

Driven by a strong pragmatic component, all work encompasses a basic energy concept which emphasises the use of local resources and clean construction processes. Both requirements aim to reduce the amount of energy required to transport materials on site and to reduce the impact the construction process could generate on the area. Priority is thus generally given to passive energy use. But besides ecological considerations, students are forced to search for solutions where small innovations have a maximum effect on the local economy, improving a building's quality both spatially and in energy use. The challenge lies in providing an appropriate quality of life from interiors to public open spaces with low-tech materials and resources. In opposition to standardised solutions, these extreme conditions oblige young designers to assess every single case in its specificity and foster a synergic perspective on sustainability and energy. ◣

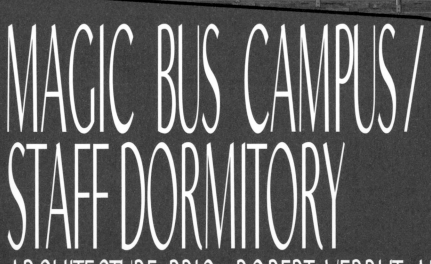

MAGIC BUS CAMPUS/
STAFF DORMITORY
ARCHITECTURE BRIO: ROBERT VERRIJT AND SHEFALI BALWANI

ENGINEER	CLIENT	PROJECT LOCATION	COMPLETION DATE
GeoScience Services: Vilas Gore	Childlink India Foundation (Magic Bus)	Karjat/Maharashtra/ India	Ongoing

01

02

03

04

ASSIGNMENT

Magic Bus is a non-governmental organisation founded in Mumbai in 1999 aspiring to create a long-term, sustained intervention of life skills development for at-risk children through recreation, play and creative expression activities. The NGO organises weekly sports and games sessions, and educational day-trips to their weekend residential camp known as the Magic Bus Centre. Mumbai-based Architecture BRIO have been asked to design the second construction phase of the centre comprising a staff dormitory, separate facilitation centres for children and corporations, and individual residential accommodations. The requirement for the dormitory was to accommodate 40 adults with sleeping arrangements on bunk beds, open and semi-open areas for dining and recreation, and a kitchen. Despite a limited construction budget, the client wished for the character of the organisation to be reflected in the architecture of the campus. ◣

LOCATION

The Magic Bus Campus is located in a small valley in the Indian countryside. Situated near a river, the sloping site is surrounded by paddy fields and small sleepy villages. The dormitory for the staff, located on top of a plateau, derives its typology from that of a colonial missionary bungalow. The linear plan of the missionary bungalow allows for an efficient way of distributing private spaces along a common veranda, where people can interact. A staircase cutting through the building mass breaks up the long passage on the ground floor. The staircase leads one down to a recreational space which is generously large. At the end of a colonnaded passage, a large shaded deck provides a spectacular view over the trees, towards the contours of the Matheran mountain range in the distance. ◣

CONCEPT

The building is an attempt to integrate design, as well as structure and building techniques, with the use of local materials in a wider socio-cultural context. The chosen construction system had to reduce the use of steel in the project yet allow the structures to remain light and blend in with the natural environment. Bamboo, being the fastest growing grass in the world and a high-yielding renewable material resource, was a complex but logical choice as the main construction material. Despite the historical prominence of bamboo in traditional building techniques, the productive use of this material is remarkably low. This is owed to limited and disappearing knowledge, and a lack of skills and basic tools. But bamboo also has the negative social connotation of being temporary and low class. This project deliberately dedicates itself to research on and the promotion of bamboo as a building material and gives hope that, with the necessary training, a desired level and sophistication in construction can be achieved. ◣

REALISATION

Large covered verandas and the narrow width of the building envelope allow for comfortably ventilated and shaded semi-indoor spaces. The bamboo enclosure creates a dialogue between the interior and the dramatically changing landscape. The screen of columns creates an ever-changing pattern of light and shadow throughout the seasons and times of the day, making the building a sensor of light. The selection of materials and building methods is optimised to decrease the weight of the building, which in turn allows the supporting columns to be sleek and elegantly dimensioned. For dormitory design, bamboo is used for floors and wall panels, and for columns to support three storeys of residential space. The construction details emphasise the lightness of the structure. A steel plate, which is embedded in a pre-cast concrete beam, connects to both the lower and upper bamboo twin-column as well as the bamboo tie beams. While this steel plate cuts through the bamboo column to make use of reverse bending, the continuity of the bamboo columns is maintained, accentuating the verticality of the structure. Combining natural and local materials with state-of-the-art technologies and material such as wood, concrete and steel, this building aspires to portray a new construction idiom – an expression of contemporary low-tech sustainable architecture. ◣

ENERGY CONCEPT

The linear plan of the building is exploited for its excellent cross ventilation and sun management to avoid the need for air conditioning. During the hot summer months, when the temperatures can rise to 40 degrees Celsius, the sun's latitude almost reaches 90 degrees Celsius. With the lower sides of the building oriented towards the west and east, the surface area that is exposed to the sun is minimised. The continuous veranda on the west, south and east sides shades the walls from sun. The exterior sandwich wall panels, consisting of bamboo and plaster, have good insulating properties. Only the long and cool north façade opens up to the surroundings with large windows. A long and narrow plan encourages cross ventilation through the rooms. The proposal for the dormitory also makes use of the large quantity of monsoon rainwater, which will be channelled through generous gutters from the rooftops and collected in tanks situated above the toilets. Any overflow is distributed to either percolation pits or to the groundwater recharge pond located near the entrance of the building. This pond is positioned in a catchment area and collects a large portion of the rainwater surface runoff coming from the hills south of the site. All waste water generated is collected and treated by a decentralised waste-water treatment system. The last two treatment basins of the system, the horizontal planted gravel filter and the polishing pond create a lush wetland and are integrated into the landscape design. The surplus waste water is used for gardening purposes. Furthermore, the thermal insulation of the composite wall panels is relatively high. Bamboo itself has high insulating properties, and the hollow cavity of bamboo improves this quality. The high strength and low weight factor of bamboo make it remarkably earthquake and cyclone resistant. ◣

GREENING THE ROMFORD RING ROAD
WHAT IF: PROJECTS LTD (GARETH MORRIS + ULRIKE STEVEN)

ENGINEER
Jacobs

CLIENT
London Borough of Havering (LBH)

PROJECT LOCATION
Romford/United Kingdom

COMPLETION DATE
In planning as of November 2008

ASSIGNMENT

What if: projects Ltd. are an East London-based art and architecture practice established in 2005. Their work focuses on urban sustainability and new ways of implementing ideas and strategies through engaging communities. The value of the land is seen as a place for humanity to re-connect with nature. In this way the natural qualities of the site become a catalyst for regeneration of the surrounding area. What if: projects Ltd. examine void spaces and the opportunities these spaces can offer to a neighbourhood, a city and beyond. Their strategies and interventions are then developed in collaboration with regeneration agencies, local authorities, art organisations, urban research bodies and the public. What if: projects Ltd. were commissioned by the London Borough of Havering to develop a creative public regeneration scheme and masterplan for the Romford Ring Road. The borough wishes to reinvent the ring road as a boulevard which reinforces and generates links between the town centre and the surrounding neighbourhoods. ◤

LOCATION

Havering is a borough on the outskirts of London with many suburban and green belt spaces. The dominant mode of transport is the car. Romford is the largest town centre in Havering and the fourth largest in London. It is one of its top 15 retail centres. The town centre is encircled by the Romford Ring Road, which was built in 1969. It connects to four arterial roads, all of which form part of the Strategic Road Network (SRN). Each arterial road joins the Romford Ring Road at a roundabout. Currently, the ring road both contains the town centre and isolates it from its immediate surroundings by creating a barrier to pedestrian movement. ◤

CONCEPT

What if: projects Ltd.'s approach to developing the Greening the Romford Ring Road project involved a masterplan and design guide. The aim is to change the public's perception of the ring road environment and involve the public in the process of change through engaging strategies and projects. For What if: projects Ltd., master planning is considered to be a process with small beginnings. They set out a list of key questions:

01

What if the countryside were linked to the town centre? What if the roundabouts became centres for culture, learning and play? What if residents did not have to climb over railings and barriers anymore? What if the Ring Road became Romford's new front garden? Now the team is developing a series of small, medium and large scale improvement projects that initiate a process of change and inform adjustments to the Romford Ring Road in the future.

S

A series of small changes - low budget proposals - aim to challenge Romford residents' perception of the ring road. These proposals look in particular at the potential of existing unused and unloved space along the ring road that could be transformed into Romford's New Front Gardens through a combination of growing projects, cultural, educational programmes and display of information about the nature beyond the town centre, walking and cycle distances.

M

A series of medium-scale projects involves the removal of existing physical and visual barriers along the ring road to allow for new access and visual connections to existing unused green spaces and places of interest. The removal of these barriers would open up spaces such as the River Rom environment, which is currently isolated by fences and barbed wire, so that it can become part of the ring road public realm. The removal of the continuous railings and the central reservation will help to slow down the traffic speed to its current limit of 30 mph and transform the ring road from an inner city motorway into a street.

L

Large change is about creating new axes into the town centre that allow easy access to nature beyond and to provide for a new sequence of public spaces that cross over the ring road. New dedicated bus and cycle lanes along the ring road, as well as cycle routes and the Romford tree-planting programme are proposed. As part of the large scale changes, What if: projects Ltd. suggest conceiving the ring road as a linear park with a unified approach to pavement surfaces, street furniture, co-ordinated signage, cycle parking and tree planting.

XL

Romford is located in the area of the East London Green Grid, which aims to provide improved access to nature from urban environments. Instead of being a barrier, could places alongside the ring road become destinations? What If: projects propose that the ring road could have a new role providing access to the green grid through the improvement of existing subways, roundabouts and street crossings and through the creation of new street crossings. New and improved places of entry to the town centre would create footfall to the edges of the ring road and benefit present and future developments. As well as becoming part of the green network, the existing roundabouts could host cultural programmes in relation to their immediate environments to complement the limited cultural programmes currently on offer in Romford. Each roundabout could be unique. ▲

public engagement projects – small scale interventions and events that aim to engage the public and test ideas. Outcomes and feedback from these projects inform the Design Guide, and the development of the pilot projects. Part three is the development of a Design Guide which aims to provide an overall vision and a tool kit for co-ordinated improvements to the Romford Ring Road public realm. The Guide will include recommendations on greening, street furniture, surface materials, signage and the integration of cycle lanes. Part four involves pilot projects – the development of a series of small-scale public engagements that start the process of change and implement the vision as outlined in the Design Guide. Small-scale projects can be implemented through simple means and require small-scale budgets. The designers propose that a larger-scale pilot project should centre on improvements to a roundabout space and associated subway network. Greening the Romford Ring Road is working toward a long-term vision of delivering a Linear Park. The ambition is to consider the ring road as a new three-kilometre-long green corridor of connecting open spaces that can accommodate areas for tree planting, places to rest and sit, areas for play, areas for art and cultural events, public spaces, and new green spaces that bring wildlife and nature to the town centre. ▲

REALISATION

The delivery of the masterplan is in progress and consists of four parts: part one involves urban analysis – mapping vacant and unused spaces around the ring road and looking into potential green routes such as cycle paths, footpaths and green corridors. Part two involves

ENERGY CONCEPT

The Greening the Romford Ring Road Masterplan and Design Guide is a strong combination of social and infrastructural measures which can dramatically improve the environment of the area at a number of levels. It aims to improve the walking and cycling environment and access to public transport. The designers also wish to reduce the number of short-distance car journeys and create an environment that can be sustained by the local population in partnership with Council services. The plan will reduce maintenance requirements of green spaces through native planting that supports local wildlife (i.e. wildflower meadows). It will also specify materials, trees and street furniture that are sustainable and can be sourced locally as part of the Design Guide, and it will encourage solar-powered street lighting. ▲

01 View of green roundabout.

02 Vacant lot. Planting seeds in the half-tonne bags of soil.

03 An inaccessible and run-down plot of housing estate turned into an oasis of green by local residents.

04 Surrounding area. Subway station near Romford Ring.

01/02

01 Sand bags within a timber-frame construction.

02 View of the surrounding settlement.

03 Construction process. The sandbags are plastered over and timber boarding is used in parts.

03

ENGINEER
Henry Herring, Aki/Axis
Consulting engineers

CLIENT
Mr. Ravi Naidoo Design
Indaba & Interactive Africa

PROJECT LOCATION
Freedom Park, Cape Town,
South Africa

COMPLETION DATE
2009

10 X 10 DESIGN INDABA
LOW-COST HOUSE
LUYANDA MPAHLWA/MMA ARCHITECTS

05/06

04 Building footprint. Maximising the usable area by minimising the building footprint as much as possible.

05 A double-storey unit was proposed as the most land-use efficient option for the design.

06 Punched windows and translucent polycarbonate sheeting are used to maximise natural light penetration and to reduce heat gain in the building.

ASSIGNMENT

In 2007 the Design Indaba invited ten local architects to design ten low-cost houses on ten sites in partnership with ten international architects, for ten families in Freedom Park, Mitchells Plein, Cape Town, South Africa. The initiative was part of the development of Freedom Park by Niall Mellon Developers with 490 units to be built. The brief for each architect has been to design a house within the limits of the Government for a 42-square-metre house. Originally paired with British Architect Will Also MMA Architects were allocated to design the house for a family of eight. The partnership with Will Alsop, however, did not materialise due to differing design approaches, and MMA proceeded with its own design concept. ◣

area is characterised by wet and windy winters and hot dry summers. ◣

CONCEPT

In responding to the 10 x 10 Housing Project, MMA sought to find solutions which also attempt to address the challenges facing South Africa in the housing sector, while exploring the possibility of sustainable and appropriate design solutions and restoring the dignity of beneficiary communities among the urban poor in South Africa. Due to the budgetary limitations given to the architects, MMA incorporated the idea of the possible growth of the house into their design proposal from the very beginning, which would allow the family to extend their home. ◣

LOCATION

Freedom Park was an informal settlement in Cape Town which is now being upgraded with Irish donor funding in partnership with the South African Government with 490 housing units. The settlement is located near the sea, south of Cape Town, on a gently sloping site. Buildings are on soft sandy soil, and the

REALISATION

The MMA proposal was the first, and the only, to be approved by the authorities. It was also the first to fulfil the budget parameters set by the client. Given the fact that the plot sizes (112 square metres) were pre-determined, MMA considered it necessary to maximise the usable area by minimising the building footprint as much as possible. A 27-square-metre footprint was achieved and a double-storey unit was proposed as the most land-use efficient option for the design. Living areas are situated on the ground floor and sleeping areas upstairs. After researching possible affordable and sustainable building methods, the result of the MMA design process was a sand-bag house made of timber-frame construction, and based on EcoBeams technology. The sandbags are plastered over and timber boarding is used in parts. This construction method represents a contemporary interpretation of indigenous building methods, which used mud/adobe with timber inlays to provide structure. Relying mostly on unskilled labour, the relatively simple sandbag construction method furthermore allowed all members of the community to be involved in the actual building process, thereby creating a sense of ownership, belonging and contribution in the participants. ◣

ENERGY CONCEPT

Tapping into the indigenous building techniques that made the traditional buildings thermally sound and comfortable to live in, the sand bags provide excellent thermal mass qualities for passive thermal control. This thermal wall concept is to insulate the building's interiors from external conditions. Sand does not allow lateral penetration of water or moisture into the interior walls. The moisture is absorbed downwards within the sandbag wall by force of gravity, thus keeping the interior dry. In the harsh, hot summer months, the thermal wall keeps the extreme heat out of the building and the warmth generated inside the building in winter is prevented from escaping. Punched windows and translucent polycarbonate sheeting are used to maximise natural light penetration and reduce heat gain. ◣

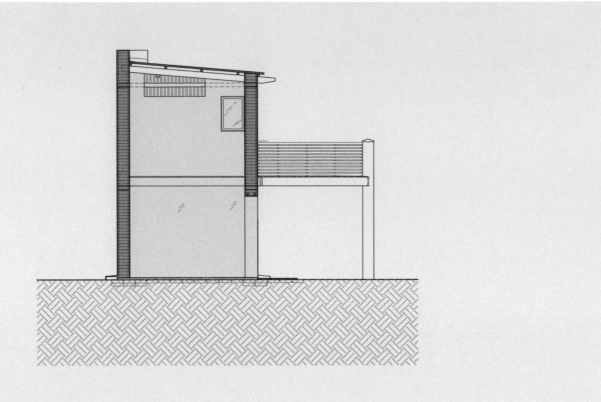

Section A - A

02

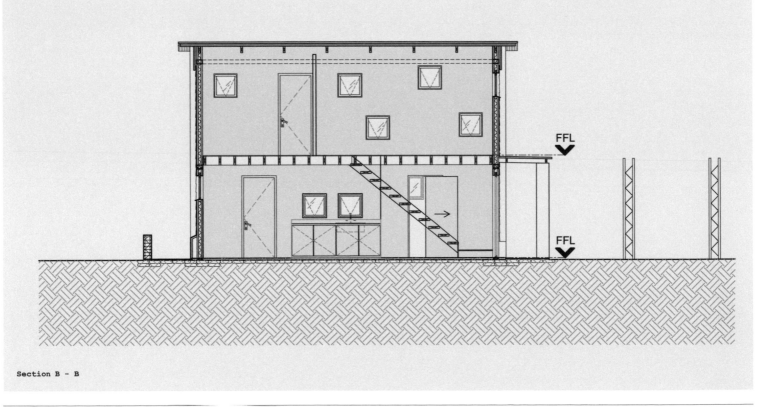

Section B - B

01 Cross section of the
10 x 10 Indaba Low Cost
House.

02 Longitudinal section.
Living areas are
situated on the ground
floor, sleeping areas on
the first floor.

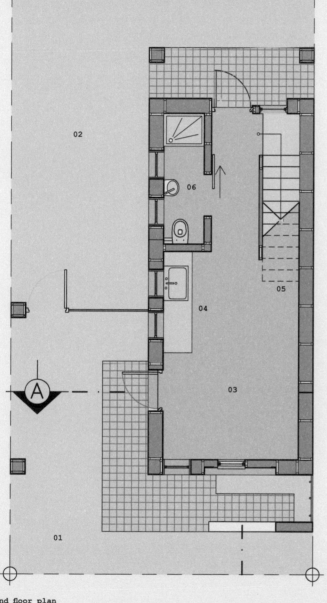

Ground floor plan

First floor plan

03 Floor plans. Maximising
the usable area by
minimising the building
footprint as much as
possible.

03.01 Entrance
03.02 Garden
03.03 Living room
03.04 Kitchenette
03.05 Dining/Study
03.06 Bathroom
03.07 Balcony
03.08 Master bedroom
03.09 Bedroom 2

CENTRE POUR LES BIEN-ÊTRE DE FEMMES

FARE STUDIO

CLIENT
AIDOS (Associazione italiana donne per lo sviluppo) Voix des Femmes

PROJECT LOCATION
Ouagadougou, Burkina Faso

COMPLETION DATE
2007

01 North elevation of the Women's Health Centre in Burkina Faso.

02 View of external walls, which are finished in brightly painted plaster.

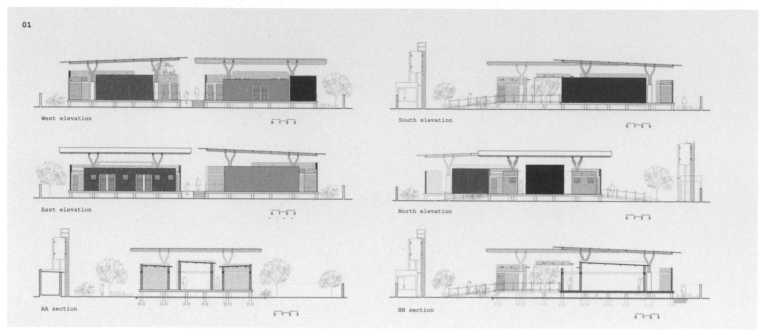

West elevation

South elevation

East elevation

North elevation

AA section

BB section

01 Elevations and sections of the buildings on site.

02 Side view of the building.

03 Perspective view.

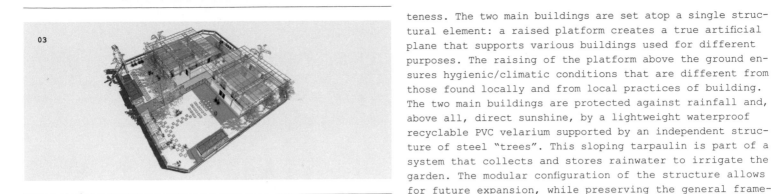

ASSIGNMENT

The Centre pour le Bien-être des Femmes (CBF) in Burkina Faso was created between 2005 and 2007 by AIDOS, an Italian NGO fighting for women's rights in developing countries. The AIDOS project, financed by the Democratici di Sinistra Political Party with a contribution from the European Commission, is one of the group's international programmes focused on combating the spread of female genital mutilation. The architectural project is a direct response to a social programme that called for the realisation of a building complex capable of hosting a variety of activities in very harsh circumstances. ◣

REALISATION

Completed in 15 months by a local builder working under the direct supervision of the architects FARE, the CBF is a functional and cost-effective answer to the needs expressed by AIDOS, while simultaneously and primarily representing a centre of meeting and identity for the entire local community. The technological and typological responses offered by the project, on par with its social objectives, represent an innovative approach to traditional local building practices, presented as the natural formal expression of the changes and new approaches promoted by AIDOS. The project privileges an integrated approach to interaction between built space and climatic-environmental conditions, based on considerations of sustainability and appropria-

LOCATION

The project, realised in a 1600-square-metre site donated to AIDOS by Ouagadougou's municipal government, is located in Sector 27, a peripheral urban area settled by a once rural population. Sector 27, one of the town's poorest suburbs, is defined by a multitude of small, spontaneously constructed mud huts and is entirely devoid of any planning regulations or basic infrastructure. ◣

CONCEPT

The project is based on the separation of the primary activities performed by the CBF into two distinct, though closely related, buildings: a training centre dedicated to activities of awareness-building and to administration and management; and a consultancy centre, used for medical visits, legal assistance and psychological counselling. The initial design was developed prior to the definition of the project site and at a time when the office possessed very little technical information about locally available technologies and materials. As a consequence, the early stages of the project were approached as a work in progress – a typological model with some clearly defined architectonic characteristics derived from climatic, environmental, technical and economic considerations and flexible and adaptable to any possible site. ◣

teness. The two main buildings are set atop a single structural element: a raised platform creates a true artificial plane that supports various buildings used for different purposes. The raising of the platform above the ground ensures hygienic/climatic conditions that are different from those found locally and from local practices of building. The two main buildings are protected against rainfall and, above all, direct sunshine, by a lightweight waterproof recyclable PVC velarium supported by an independent structure of steel "trees". This sloping tarpaulin is part of a system that collects and stores rainwater to irrigate the garden. The modular configuration of the structure allows for future expansion, while preserving the general framework of the building. The building walls are constructed using compressed dry-stacked clay bricks made on site using a rough mixture of earth, cement and water. The buildings are covered by corrugated aluminium and translucent decking that allows natural light to filter into the interior, reducing the need for artificial illumination. The space between the steel roof and the velarium and the open cavity beneath the platform, together with the exterior openings fitted with operable glass fins, all help to improve the natural ventilation of interior spaces and drastically reduce the need for mechanical air conditioning. The outside walls, devoid of any openings, are finished in brightly painted plaster with the local NGO's slogan, translated into five languages. The exterior space, similar to the interior, is designed as an open area to be used by the entire community. The garden is a micro environment that surrounds the structure and takes advantage of the shade provided by the building and trees and the humidity produced by the plants. A grass layer reduces the effects of erosion, while various species from western and sub-Saharan Africa have been planted with the twofold intention of creating shade and promoting the return of indigenous vegetation. ◣

ENERGY CONCEPT

Temperature control, perhaps the most significant climatic issue, has strongly influenced the overall design of the project. The adopted strategy also includes a carefully studied building orientation that reduces the effects of hot wind and takes advantage of mutual overshading, the shading of heavy material against direct exposure to the sun as well as the extensive use of operable windows and the use of transitional spaces, such as verandas or patios, to separate enclosed areas. Given the lack of water and power in the area, the centre is fully independent. Integrated systems for the systematic control of energy consumption are accompanied by energy self-production, using largely renewable resources. Water is provided by a newly drilled and dedicated well, and photovoltaic cells have been installed along the perimeter wall, reducing the use of the electrical generator. These simple steps affect both personal behaviour and collective responsibility: the elimination of mechanical air conditioning (limited to medical rooms in order to assure filtered air) is perhaps the project's most important achievement in terms of environmental sustainability. Since its completion, the CBF has become a focal point for the rapid development of a wide range of new activities. The first direct effects of the suburb's newly acquired visibility can be seen in the municipality's decision to build a new road, to create electrical and water supply connections, to construct a new maternity clinic and to donate a once empty field to women living in Sector 27 for use as an income-generating self-cultivated vegetable garden. ◣

POLITICAL EQUATOR II
ESTUDIO TEDDY CRUZ

PROJECT LOCATION
San Diego, USA
Tijuana, Mexico

COMPLETION DATE
2007

01/02/03/04

01/ Impressions of the mobile
02/ symposium on the move.
03/
04/

05 The critical observation of local zones of conflict transforms the Tijuana–San Diego region into a laboratory from which to reflect current politics of migration, labour and surveillance.

06 Producing support systems for dwelling in the informal urbanism of Tijuana.

07

ASSIGNMENT

As the follow-up to its 2006 predecessor, the Political Equator II was a trans-border public event held in November 2007. In collaboration with Tránsito(ry) Público/Public(o) Transit(orio) it was choreographed as a mobile symposium, a conversation on the intersection between sociopolitical and natural domains. Traversing the borders between the United States and Mexico it sought to explore the conflict between transcontinental borders and the natural and social ecologies they interrupt and seek to erase. ▲

LOCATION

The three-day, event-based itinerary follows travels from Los Angeles to San Diego to Tijuana, and back again. A provocative series of events and interventions was hosted by major cultural institutions, neighbourhood-based NGOs, and independent alternative spaces, eventually crossing over into the no man's land of the border zone itself, where the Tijuana River symbolises the conflicts these collaborative practices seek to expose and engage. ▲

CONCEPT

The field of operations represented by the collectives of architects and urbanists brought together for the Political Equator II traces an invisible trajectory across a political divide running along a south to north axis, along which emergent Latin American practices of intervention simultaneously engage the politics of the environment and policies that are shaping contemporary cities. Against the backdrop of global warming, being continuously understood solely as an environmental crisis and not as a cultural crisis, the Political Equator II saw the need to produce different ways to re-engage the public and the meaning of research in empowering new communities of practice. It tried to promote and foster a renewed politics of environmental activism, searching for effective paths to sustainability worldwide. ▲

REALISATION

The Political Equator II has been conceived as a way of re-defining conventional protocols of the traditional research conference, generally conceived as exclusive and highly specialised, opening it up, instead, as an experimental platform to examine new configurations of practice and public participation, amplifying the debate and relationship between cultural institutions and communities. In this context, the event directly evolved out of Teddy Cruz's work at the San Diego-Tijuana border, where the architect sought the exposure of conflict as the main operational instrument to redefine architectural practice. This border territory has been the laboratory within which to reflect on the current territorial politics of migration, labour and surveillance, the tensions between sprawl and density, formal and informal urbanisms and the division between enclaves of mega wealth and sectors of poverty. The Political Equator II takes this research from a local to a global scale, connecting the Tijuana-San Diego border with other geographies of global conflict, producing new correspondences between the local and the international. Essential to this effort has been the desire to draw the public across these geographic scales, in order to experience directly the very juxtapositions and conflicts this research is trying to engage. The upcoming Political Equator III project will research a more meaningful socio-political and economic role for architecture, suggesting that no advances in environmental sustainability and building design can occur without reorganising existing political structures, economic resources and social capital in neighbourhoods worldwide. ▲

UKUKULA CENTRE
ARG DESIGN: VERENA GRIPS

ENGINEER
Henry Fagan, Cape Town, South Africa

LANDSCAPE DESIGN
Louise Cheetham

CLIENT
Architecture for Humanity, San Francisco, USA, for Football for Hope (strategic alliance between FIFA and streetfootballworld)

PROJECT LOCATION
Khayelitsha, Cape Town, South Africa

COMPLETION DATE
2010

01

01 Section illustrating the holistic water management system.

02 Positioned along a pedestrian road, the Ukukula Centre is integrated in an existing public network.

03 East elevation.

04 West elevation.

05 Cross section.

ASSIGNMENT

The official campaign of the 2010 FIFA World Cup in South Africa will carry the name Football for Hope – 20 Centres for 2010. The concept of the campaign is to build 20 Football for Hope Centres between 2008 and 2010 to benefit 20 disadvantaged African communities. It is intended to be the driving force behind a global network of non-governmental organisations, developing projects on the ground in which football is the common denominator. The objective of the Football for Hope movement is to bring together, support, advise and strengthen sustainable social and human development programmes in the areas of peace promotion, children's rights and education, health promotion, anti-discrimination, social integration and the environment. These programmes must be aimed at children and young people and use football as an instrument to promote participation and dialogue. Competitors were challenged to design a small-sized pitch (20 metres x 40 metres) with surrounding space for spectators as well as classrooms and media, health, conference and educational facilities that can offer young Africans the chance to further their scholastic and sporting education while providing them with health and social services. Participants are challenged to incorporate the needs of the community and to employ sustain-able and/or local building materials and construction methods to achieve their design. There is the potential to create shared services to the community at large, including access to water, power and other support services. ▲

CONCEPT

To be able to adapt the concept to any chosen site, the built form was conceptualised as a starting block for future development: the roof structure of the ground floor is structurally able to support another floor above it. The construction material is primarily sand, which is sourced from the site. All materials are low energy, water and energy saving systems are integrated, and waste collection areas are part of the layout. The urban space around the centre features creative and colourful floor patterns interspersed with trees that draw people toward the space. A kind of urban amphitheatre is created via the angular geometry of the centre, a space from which soccer matches or movies can be displayed using the light tower as a projection backdrop. The multi-use health/education/trading spaces invite users into the centre and onto the playing field. The field space is drained into a detention basin that doubles as a vegetable garden where food can be grown for a soup kitchen. Through activities of all kinds, the centre is supervised and people of all ages are brought together during leisure time. UKUKULA aims to bring football - and hope - to the urban realm, sparking a social regeneration in the community and guiding Khayelitsha's children into an uplifting future. ▲

LOCATION

The living conditions in South Africa's townships are challenging in many ways: open space is often limited or located on the exposed periphery. The landscape, although vibrant with life, is dominated by high density settlements of corrugated iron shacks and homes in bad condition, insufficient infrastructure, and high unemployment and crime rates. Uplifting entertainment and positive contributions are needed – especially for the young. ARG Design's "Football for Hope" concept integrates football into the heart of Khayelitsha, the largest township in the disadvantaged areas of Cape Town. It is designed to be woven into a high intensity pedestrian route with guaranteed exposure. Using shipping containers, the central concept around the built form is a tower of light that can be seen from the surrounding neighbourhood. The name Ukukula is from the Xhosa language, meaning "rising above" or "hope". ◣

REALISATION

The Ukukula Centre is conceptualised as a community building, integrated into the pedestrian network. Its maximal exposure and the creation of public urban space on the one hand, and the semi-public activities in the protected and rather introverted heart of the centre on the other, generate different degrees of interaction. The dynamically shaped shop/office element forms the interface between these zones; the tower creates the landmark and is illuminated at night. The pedestrian flow is guided either along the shop front or into the building; it presents itself as both inviting and protective. The first of both larger volumes offers space for seminars and teamwork. The other one contains change rooms and toilets next to the health rooms within and external access. Both buildings are individually shaped and covered by a flat roof at a height of 3.2 metres. These buildings stand out as being painted in a warm red colour which marks the optimistic and constructive atmosphere created around the centre and highlights its significance in the community. All inner façades create an open atmosphere by large openings, and visual connections between in- and outdoor areas stimulate interaction, whereas externally the building presents a solid façade with narrow vertical openings. Safety lines are planned on both narrow ends of the entrance to ensure safety at night. To allow for future growth, all foundations and walls are structured to carry a second storey, the roof construction can be used as a floor, a staircase can be added in the tower, and the external pergola can be simply covered and used as a walkway. The donated shipping containers, staged above each other, will create the tower and can be modified to a unique light installation, viewing screen, outlook, technical hub and water store. As the building is structured primarily with locally produced eco-beams filled with sandbags, a large part of the construction can be done in cooperation with the community. Collective building processes have long traditions in African cultures and support the development of self-esteem, pride and awareness of the local neighbourhood. Engaging and empowering the community create identification with the built environment and build responsible relationships. ◣

ENERGY CONCEPT

The Ukukula project has a number of sustainable features: there is water saving via rainwater collection through catchment systems from roof gutters into water tanks on the first floor of the tower from where it gets pumped into toilet tanks. Solar energy is used to illuminate the building, light box and external areas. A solar water heater on the tower roof heats water for showers. Natural cross ventilation in all rooms and massive walls allow for thermal comfort. A double-skin roof creates an enclosed air buffer in winter or ventilation under the heated roof sheet in summer to avoid the need for electrical air conditioning. Narrow vertical windows allow maximum indirect daylight without glaring. With respect to the building materials, there is an eco-beam system – a locally produced lightweight low-cost construction element – with infills from sandbags, filled on site by local workers. This provides excellent thermal and acoustic stability, a short construction period and high durability for user comfort. The use of locally produced materials avoids high CO_2 emissions through transport, and long-life materials avoid high maintenance costs. The centre has a storm water drainage and detention basin which slow down run-off from the artificial turf surface into a detention basin area feeding a nutrient-rich vegetable garden. Social sustainability is encouraged by the centre: the implementing partner (an NGO) will use the centre to encourage strong integration of the local neighbourhood via activities such as a nutrition programme, vegetable garden, raising awareness for waste treatment and skill training. ◣

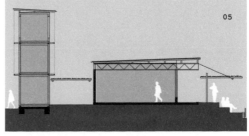

MAKE IT RIGHT
MAKE IT RIGHT FOUNDATION

PROJECT LOCATION
Lower Ninth Ward, New Orleans, USA

COMPLETION DATE
Ongoing

01
Areal view of Lower Ninth Ward in New Orleans with the Pink Project. 150 different, temporary model houses were created by GRAFT architects out of lightweight aluminum frames, covered in vibrant pink fabric and placed around the site as placeholders for future residences. The idea to use the color pink was developed by actor Brad Pitt. The aim is to attract both attention and investment.

01 Rendering of building designed by Kieran Timberlake architects.

02 View of the built house by Kieran Timberlake architects. Variations to the exterior fit-out, including photovoltaic panels, sunscreens, grade level storage and an expand-able rainwater collection system, allow the house to accomodate the varying needs and budgets of a range of homeowners.

03 Night-view of house designed by GRAFT architects. The houses use the cradle to cradle philosophy and received LEED platinum certi-fication.

04 View of the house with surround site. The building is made from prefabricated modular units, con-structed off-site.

ASSIGNMENT

The Make It Right Foundation (MIR) was founded by Brad Pitt to help a number of New Orleans residents following the destruction caused by Hurricane Katrina in 2005. Driven by the U.S. government's slow reaction to the initial emergency and ongoing crisis, and after a series of community meetings with New Orleans residents, Brad Pitt commissioned a group of internationally acclaimed architects to help rebuild the impoverished Lower Ninth Ward, one of the neighbourhoods hit hardest by the hurricane. They were asked to build 150 affordable, environmentally sound houses over the coming years. ◣

REALISATION

The Make it Right core team assembled by Pitt includes experts such as William McDonough + Partners, a world leader in environmental architecture; Cherokee Gives Back Foundation, the non-profit arm of Cherokee, a firm that specialises in remediation and sustainable redevelopment of environmentally impaired properties; Graft, an innovative architecture firm that Pitt has collaborated with on projects around the world; as well as Trevor Neilson and Nina Killeen, advisors to the Jolie-Pitt Foundation. This core team is working in tandem with leaders of a local, neighbourhood-led coalition of not-for-profits, and

CONCEPT

The Mission of Make It Right is to be a catalyst for redevelopment of the Lower Ninth Ward. It is to build a neighbourhood of safe and healthy homes that are inspired by cradle-to-cradle thinking, with an emphasis on high-quality design, while preserving the spirit of the community's culture. ◣

LOCATION

The Lower Ninth Ward of New Orleans is one of the richest cultural communities in the United States and was, until Hurricane Katrina in August 2005, a crossroads of families, music and social interaction in New Orleans. ◣

MIR's goal is to join the history of this tradition with creative new architectural solutions mindful of environmental and personal safety concerns in order to encourage both the evolution of aesthetic distinctiveness and the conscientious awareness of natural surroundings. ◣

has expanded to include renowned local, national and international architecture firms, to ensure that the focus on – and commitment to – the Lower Ninth Ward is demonstrably diverse and reflective of Brad Pitt's dedication to giving this critical neighbourhood access to the best expertise available. In keeping with Make It Right's overarching priority to work in cooperation with former residents of the Lower Ninth Ward, the approach to new home design began directly with the homeowners themselves. Because local cultural influences gave rise to the pre-Katrina architecture so emblematic of the area, preserving that identity remains vital in reclaiming the spirit of the neighbourhood.

ENERGY CONCEPT

The four main guiding principles for the designs are safety, affordability, sustainability and high-quality design. The Make It Right team produced a set of guidelines for the houses that set metrics for the final design to ensure that the specific goals of the organisations were met. All architects were each asked to design a 1200-square-foot house for about $150,000 with Make It Right to help with the financing. The houses had to be built five to eight feet off the ground, with a front porch and three bedrooms. In doing so, the team is also using cradle-to-cradle thinking to guide and inspire design and materials selected for the new homes. Cradle-to-cradle thinking suggests that everything we create can contribute positively to society, the economy and the environment. This thinking was developed and popularised by architect William McDonough and chemist Michael Braungart in their 2002 book, *Cradle to Cradle: Remaking the Way We Make Things*. ◣

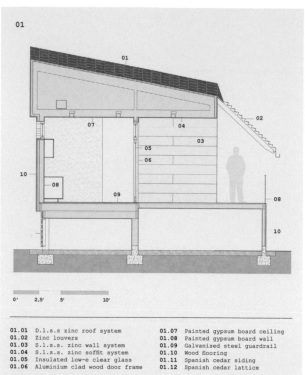

01

01.01 D.l.s.s zinc roof system
01.02 Zinc louvers
01.03 S.l.s.s. zinc wall system
01.04 S.l.s.s. zinc soffit system
01.05 Insulated low-e clear glass
01.06 Aluminium clad wood door frame
01.07 Painted gypsum board ceiling
01.08 Painted gypsum board wall
01.09 Galvanised steel guardrail
01.10 Wood flooring
01.11 Spanish cedar siding
01.12 Spanish cedar lattice

02

01 Cross section of the building designed by
Trahan Architects. As the roof began to evolve
from practical form and function, it transitioned into a highperformance component that
acts as a shading device, rainscreen, water
collector, solar energy collector and solar
water heater.

02 View of building process.

03 Front view of building by Trahan Architects.
As the roof began to evolve from practical
form and function, it transitioned into a
high performance component that acts as a
shading device, rainscreen, water collector,
solar energy collector and solar water heater.

04 Back view.

01

CHAPTER 04

TOMORROW NEVER DIES

Last but not least, the concluding chapter, Tomorrow Never Dies, offers challenging architectonic and urbanistic design examples of the moment, and also provokes propositions on how our future environment might look. Caught between the present and the future, the realistic and the utopian, these projects deliberately push the envelope in their creativity and optimism. What we witness here stretches from the down-to-earth winning pavilion of the Solar Decathlon competition in the United States, to a poetic, butterfly-covered Garden & Nectar Building in Colombia by Madrid-based architects HUSOS, from Laurie Chetwood's vast and equally sculptural sail for harnessing wind power to OMA's vision for the future of the North Sea and Terrefuge's colossal master plan for a self-sufficient New York City.

LUKAS FEIREISS IN CONVERSATION
WITH CHRIS LUEBKEMAN PART 2

UNFOLDING TOMORROW/THRIVING FOR FICTIONS OF OUR MULTIPLE FUTURES

IT'S VERY IMPORTANT TO REALISE THAT THIS IS THE MOMENT IN TIME IN WHICH WE CAN TURN TO THE BIGGER WORLD AND BRING ARCHITECTURE AND PLAN-NING BACK INTO THE REALM OF PUBLIC DISCOURSE.

LH: In order not to repeat the tragic story of the black-smith, the architect today has to take a stand — in particular against the backdrop of the undeniablerole the building industry plays in advancing global warming. Is it naive to believe that it's actually the city planners, architects and engineers who will take over the role of the world saviour, that the battle for the future will be won or lost within the urban realm?

CL: I think architects and engineers would love to be seen as the saviours of tomorrow! Everyone wants to be relevant. We all do. I think that architects, engineers and city planners are as important today as they were in previous times. We had these opportunities again and again over time to address the context of the moment. I think it's not just the role of architects but also of politicians. If a transparent rule of law is not introduced to the majority of countries in the world, we will continue to see depression and atrocities that will blind any efforts at planning. If we don't see a more equitable distribution of wealth and the reduction of greed, we will continue to see social upheaval and probably more violent social upheaval in those countries which are considered stable. There's also an economic aspect to the battle of the future, which makes it irrelevant whether architects and engineers draw pretty pictures and make beautiful buildings. I think there's the huge element which is the human condition, which architects, engineers and planners have not included in their calculations. They will nonetheless have to deal with the results and outcome of this omission. But the aforementioned is just a long way to say that I believe architects, engineers and planners are key parts of the success of our species on the planet, but they are by far not the only ones. If anything, they need to be far more active in politics and in their communities. Architects should not be talking to themselves but to others, so that politicians or chairmen around the world also begin to grasp that a healthy city and a healthy built environment are good for business. If they, however, continue to simply talk to themselves, and furthermore speak a language that nobody else does, then they can be as clever as they want but nobody will ever listen to them. The need to communicate to the general public is one of the greater challenges architects, engineers and planners have to face today and in the future. I think it's very important to realise that this is the moment in time in which we can turn to the bigger world and bring architecture and planning back into the realm of public discourse. ▸

LF: One tool you've recently provided for advancing the critical reflection of these implications is a collection of cards focused on why and for whom our world is changing. This box set of 189 cards, conceived by your Foresight, Innovation and Incubation team at Arup, entitled "Drivers of Change" discusses topics like energy, waste, climate change, water, demographics, urbanisation and poverty — most of which we have been discussing so far. What are the overall structure and intention of this card set?

CL: The intention is quite simple. It was to find a way to help participants in our workshops articulate what they felt was driving change for them. It started off as a very simple exercise of asking literally thousands of people again and again the question: what is driving change for you? First we were just listening, then we started to take these answers and catalogue them. Interestingly enough, certain patterns emerged from what people thought would be driving change, no matter whether it was in a city in Africa or in Australia, whether it was in Shanghai, San Francisco or Copenhagen. The topics that were coming up again and again at the top of the list were energy, waste, climate change, water, demographics and urbanisation. We called them the "big six". Then in further conversation, poverty came up as one of the most fundamental drivers of change. Poverty manifests itself not just at the base of the pyramid in countries such as India or China or the African nations, but everywhere. The impoverished are truly everywhere in the world. We took these issues that people felt were driving change and researched and asked further what they really mean and where they intersect. Take, for example, the

we might not think of every day, but are very crucial in certain parts of the world. Later, the cards developed a life of their own; we used them in workshops and printed over 20,000 copies, of which we gave 10,000 copies to them all over the world to make sure that all of our staff were thinking about what was driving change. This way we tried to make sure that they were ready to talk to our clients and to help them think about change, to make them eventually into better clients. If we are thinking about the problems we're facing together, then we will demand better solutions in anticipation of the changes which are coming. ◥

LF: What I find particularly intriguing about this set of cards is the fact that it doesn't follow any linear narration like a book, for example. Instead, it offers multiple readings and anticipates multiple future scenarios. But coming to an end of our conversation, I would like to address your various professional backgrounds. As I understand, you are trained not only as an architect and a civil engineer but also as a geologist. The Greek term geology literally means "to talk about the earth". The field of geology encompasses the overall study of Earth materials (composition, structure, physical properties, dynamics, history) and the processes by which they are formed, moved and changed. To what extent has this academic background influenced your work as architect and engineer?

CL: That's a really good question that no one has ever asked me before. Well, I studied geology because of my grandfather. He was an inventor. A very smart man, who

THIS WAY WE TRIED TO MAKE SURE THAT THEY WERE READY TO TALK TO OUR CLIENTS AND TO HELP THEM TO THINK ABOUT CHANGE, TO MAKE THEM EVENTUALLY INTO BETTER CLIENTS.

case when a couple of years ago during a horrible cold spell in winter, energy companies started to turn off the energy provided to an entire region because the locals weren't paying the bills. This is a frightening as well as fascinating example of the chaining of energy and poverty. The question arises: can you afford to pay your energy bill if you don't have a fixed income – in particular with energy costs getting higher and higher and higher? Ultimately, these cards became a way in which to pick out 25 issues to force us all to reflect on aspects

loved geology and civil engineering but never finished university. He went straight to work. I guess I finished his degrees for him. But the thing I love about geology is that no matter where you go in the world, you have something to look at because the earth always has a story to tell. You just have to be open to read it. This is exactly what a geologist has to learn. You have to be a detective who has the imagination and the openness to understand the story with all the clues around your feet and in front of your eyes.

I always loved the idea of the planetary detective who tries to get a hand on forces that are way beyond comprehension. Take, for example, the forces and the heat that make an earthquake, the grinding of little snowflakes turning into ice or even a glacier over eons of time. This is just beyond one's comprehension, and yet the evidence is right there before us. For me, it's also deeply humbling to look at the planet around us and to know that no matter what we do as Homo sapiens, the planet will still be here, nature will still be here. On the one hand it's very comforting to know that despite the massive changes we are bringing to this planet, nature will still survive and the planet will turn as it has done over millions of years. On the other hand, it's very terrifying to think that Homo sapiens might not survive as long. But, coming back to your question, I guess that I take the geological part and mix it with the architect-humanist and the engineer-analyst and then try to use those trajectories for the storytelling of yesterday, today and tomorrow. After all, I'm an eternal optimist. I think humans have an amazing capacity for handling problems on many scales. And as deep as the challenges are that we are creating for ourselves, they might also hold an opportunity for the human brain and spirit to overcome them, to work with them and really and truly to embrace them. ◣

I ALWAYS LOVED THE IDEA OF THE PLANETARY DETECTIVE WHO TRIES TO GET A HAND ON FORCES THAT ARE WAY BEYOND COMPREHENSION.

PROTOTYPE FOR A GARDEN BUILDING WITH HOST AND NECTAR PLANTS FOR CALI'S BUTTERFLIES

HUSOS: DIEGO BARAJAS AND CAMILO GARCÍA WITH BIOLOGIST FRANCISCO AMARO

CLIENT	PROJECT LOCATION	COMPLETION DATE
Taller Croquis	Cali, Colombia	Ongoing

01 Multi-purpose covered terrace for leisure and working activities.

01

ASSIGNMENT

Madrid-based Husos architects were approached by a small business atelier that concentrates on the production of handmade clothes to design a working and living space. The programme of activities required within the project included a shop and exhibition space; an atelier space for textile painting, processing and storage; an office; a kitchen and dining space for the people working at the atelier; and two housing units with at least two bedrooms each. At a local level, a need was perceived for the shop to externalise its business and become more visible within the city. The clients also required that the building process be adapted to the financial capacity of their small company so they would not have to apply for hefty loans and mortgages. This meant construction had to be carried out in stages, growing organically in line with the clients' business. ◢

LOCATION

Cali is a tropical city in Colombia with an annual average temperature of 24 degrees Celsius. One of its most outstanding physical characteristics has traditionally been its lush and diverse vegetation, making it into a spontaneous garden city. The province of Valle del Cauca, where Cali is located, covers only two per cent of the country's total surface area, but is one of the richest regions in Colombia in terms of species variety, accounting for 25 per cent to 45 per cent of the entire country's biodiversity. ◢

CONCEPT

The project is a prototype for a garden building and a first step in activating a network of environmentally aware gardeners among the population of the city of Cali. The Garden Building for Host and Nectar Plants for Cali's Butterflies (GBHNPCB) not only houses living spaces, production spaces and a shop, but also works as an indicator of an ecosystem's biodiversity by stimulating the presence of butterflies from the region through the use of plants that host and produce nectar to feed them. Butterflies are not only one of the most effective bio-indicators, with their presence or absence being a sign of an ecosystem's environ-

01–05
The programme of activities
within the project include
a shop and exhibition space;
an atelier space for textile
painting, processing and
storage; an office; a kitchen
and dining space for the
people working at the atelier;
and two housing units with
at least two bedrooms each.

02/03/04/05

mental quality and biodiversity, but are also particularly important in this region, which contains the largest diversity of butterflies in the world. At the same time, the project relates the private concerns of an expanding small business with the public interests of the city. The whole project was planned as a means of promoting the multiple symbiotic relationships between the city of Cali and the client, acknowledging each of these as entities operating at several different scales, from the very local to the global. ◣

ENERGY CONCEPT

The project consists of two complementary components: one is the GBHNPCB, the physical infrastructure designed to be built in stages, which benefits the immediate surroundings through its conception as a vertical garden. The building is, furthermore, connected to local flora and fauna and also as a structure that generates comfortable conditions inside thanks to its porous and open façade, which facilitates natural ventilation across all floors and collects rainwater to irrigate the plants. The other is Proyecto Cali, an independent, non-profit entity, created by the architects

REALISATION

The fragile economic context in which the work was developed led to spatial solutions that were able to adapt to these unstable and uncertain conditions, and also to devise a construction process that could be carried out in stages. The project had to be conceived from the beginning as a structure under ongoing construction but at the same time finished at every stage. The GBHNPCB is composed of two main elements: the detached façade – a large metal latticework box where climbing plants can grow to host and feed the butterflies – and horizontal dislocated floor slabs, which together respond to bio- and socio-environmental aspects. The entire steel structure was built during the initial construction stage. The ground and first floors were completed and made habitable to get the most productive part of the programme underway, while leaving the second and third floor beams and columns exposed, enabling the space to be used as a multi-purpose covered terrace for leisure and working activities until the start of the next building stage. The building's design provides multiple visual links both between its interior spaces and from the outside in, with the aim of re-creating and preserving a vertical version of the hybrid use of public and private spaces so characteristic of the traditional home/business combination in the area. In Cali there is a fluid relationship at ground level between life on the streets and inside the houses, especially in the most old-fashioned neighbourhoods. ◣

along with biologist Francisco Amaro. While the GBHNPCB is a spatial infrastructure or platform, Proyecto Cali is an entity whose original goal is to develop the garden façade, but its main objective is to act as a long-term interdisciplinary entity helping to promote research and action-awareness strategies around the importance of protecting the great natural biodiversity that still exists in the area. It is currently working on the creation of a network of environmentally aware gardeners by inviting the neighbourhood's inhabitants and the atelier's clients and friends. Proyecto Cali aims to take advantage of the continuous flow of visitors to the atelier to provide information about biodiversity and publicise other issues related to urban development in Cali, seeking to join forces with local environmental activists and to promote the valuable work done by local researchers. The GBHNPCB is a clear commitment to a type of urban growth and densification that allows for the city's network of green spaces to be extended while also strengthening the links between the city and its biogeographic region. ◣

04

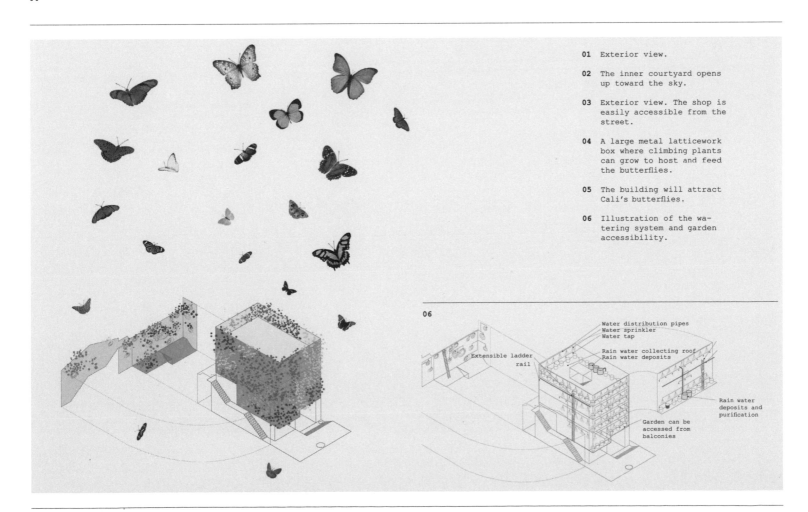

01 Exterior view.

02 The inner courtyard opens up toward the sky.

03 Exterior view. The shop is easily accessible from the street.

04 A large metal latticework box where climbing plants can grow to host and feed the butterflies.

05 The building will attract Cali's butterflies.

06 Illustration of the watering system and garden accessibility.

06

Extensible ladder rail

Water distribution pipes
Water sprinkler
Water tap
Rain water collecting roof
Rain water deposits

Rain water deposits and purification

Garden can be accessed from balconies

CUMULUS
BÜRO SMAQ – SABINE MÜLLER, ANDREAS QUEDNAU

01

ENGINEER	CLIENT	PROJECT LOCATION	COMPLETION DATE
Buro Happold	Oslo Municipality	Oslo, Norway	In progress – expected completion 2014

01 Bus terminal seen from entry to the subway.
02 New public spaces in the sustainable city.

191
CHAPTER 04

TOMORROW NEVER DIES

ASSIGNMENT

"Oslo shall be a capital city in sustainable development, characterised by economic, social and cultural growth according to nature's ability to sustain that growth ecologically. We shall pass on the city to the next generation in a better environmental condition than we ourselves inherited it. Oslo shall be one of the world's most environmentally friendly and sustainable capital cities" (Vision of the City of Oslo). The brief requested strategies and designs for a 5.5-hectare sustainable city for around 500 residents and a new public space. Architects were asked to take account of technical environmental performance (air quality, noise, water quality, microclimate, etc.) in the design to create a quality urban space for a run-down area. This involved different levels: density and open spaces, a programmatic mix and intensity, quality and management of the public domain and solutions for how new public spaces can activate social life and integrate different social, economic and ethnic groups. Architects were asked to present ideas for architecture and public spaces that give the area a new identity – architecturally, spatially and socially – and put it back on the Oslo city map. ▲

LOCATION

A declining, multi-ethnic and neglected urban borough in the city of Oslo, Norway. ▲

TOMORROW NEVER DIES

CONCEPT

The project takes environmental dynamics as a starting point to conceive social spaces. Ecological measures and the public realm are tackled at the same time. It simultaneously engages two domains that are usually discussed separately.

In a location of high precipitation, the project Cumulus harnesses the natural water cycle to generate different social spaces in the following ways:
- It harvests rain to flush toilets and run the washing machines of communal laundrettes, enhancing communication between residents.
- It initiates the yearly event of "Grorud Waterfalls" to reintroduce the site as a destination for all inhabitants of Oslo.
- It turns the public plaza into an ice-skating surface in winter to create a non-commercial and pleasurable opportunity to play, rest and encounter other inhabitants in the public realm.
- It drains the melting ice surface into the adjoining wetlands and Alna River, providing wildlife and gardeners with watering sites.
- At the level of individual buildings, the collected rainwater is used to create water gardens on the intermediate rooftop and to reflect rare sunlight into the apartments.
- It establishes an urban space that is open to the environment and its weather conditions. At the same time it enhances an open and diversified social structure.
- L-shaped dwellings with different sizes maximise light and air in the interiors and attract a mix of income groups and new users.
- New public programmes (cultural, sport and educational) are introduced. These programmes are arranged as a loose aggregate. Thus a large part of public space remains open to use by anyone. ▲

ENERGY CONCEPT

The project's innovation is to turn a sustainable water cycle into a locally relevant narrative. All measures thus focus on narrative quality, visibility, and social use-value. In terms of technology, the project will install a sustainable water cycle for the site which allows for the saving of potable water, re-use of the rain water on site and applies Sustainable Urban Drainage Systems (SUDS) to keep the rainwater in the catchment area. It is envisaged to create as many porous surfaces as possible all over the site in order to promote the infiltration of rainwater into the ground rather than to collect it and to discharge it into the nearest water course. Porous surfaces, swales and filter layers below hard surfaces will be created in car park or pedestrian areas. The rainwater from the sealed areas on site (approx. 10,000 square metres of rooftops and approx. 4000 square metres above the underground car park) is to be collected, stored and reused for toilet flushing, washing machines and for the creation of the ice-rink area during the winter months. The yearly rainfall for Oslo is about 750 millimetres; Oslo has a humid continental climate with the rainfall fairly evenly distributed all year round. The rainwater that is not required for re-use on the development, as well as the melting water from the ice rink, shall be kept in the surroundings of the area as much as possible. This measure ensures that the rivers are not charged with large amounts of additional water during wet seasons and during the snowmelt in spring, which might cause flooding further downstream.

SUDS replicate the natural drainage patterns of an area prior to development. Rainwater is allowed to infiltrate naturally into the ground and move into the natural waterways. For the Cumulus project, filter strips, swales, pervious pavements, infiltration basins will be implemented. Swales are open trenches or ditches which run across site to transport water away from the built areas while allowing it to soak into the ground naturally. With the Cumulus project, these will be used to distribute rainfall into the surrounding wetland areas (in conjunction with conventional underground drainage under road areas). The swales will be narrow or wide strips, which are depressed into the landscaping, and have a sand and gravel base. They provide a natural route for the water to flow along, as well as some filtration. The project's desired landmark qualities have to be considered together with its environmentally sustainable approach. Experts for sustainability and water were introduced to the design team. ▲

REALISATION

During the process, certain requirements of the brief were specified and emphasised. Landmark qualities and sustainability: The project's desired landmark qualities have to be considered together with its environmentally sustainable approach. Experts for sustainability and water were introduced to the design team. Non-commercial public programme: Workshops with neighbourhood representatives, representatives of the Ministry for Infrastructure, the city and local municipality, the transportation company and the site owners were held to discuss, invent and negotiate new, non-commercial programmes. Regional cooperation and integration: The plan for the revitalisation of the Alna River was discussed and integrated into the project. Role model function: Universities in Norway and abroad were introduced to the project. The project should become part of Oslo's 2014 building exhibition. ▲

01 Miniature skyscrapers in-
troduce an unusual scale.

02/ Cumulus elevation
03 and section.

04 Approaching Cumulus. Rain
gutters and drainage pipes
on the façade coin the
image of the architecture.

02

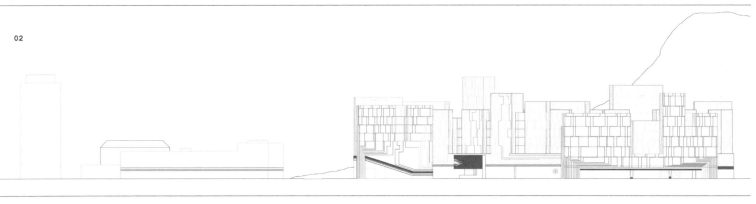

03

04

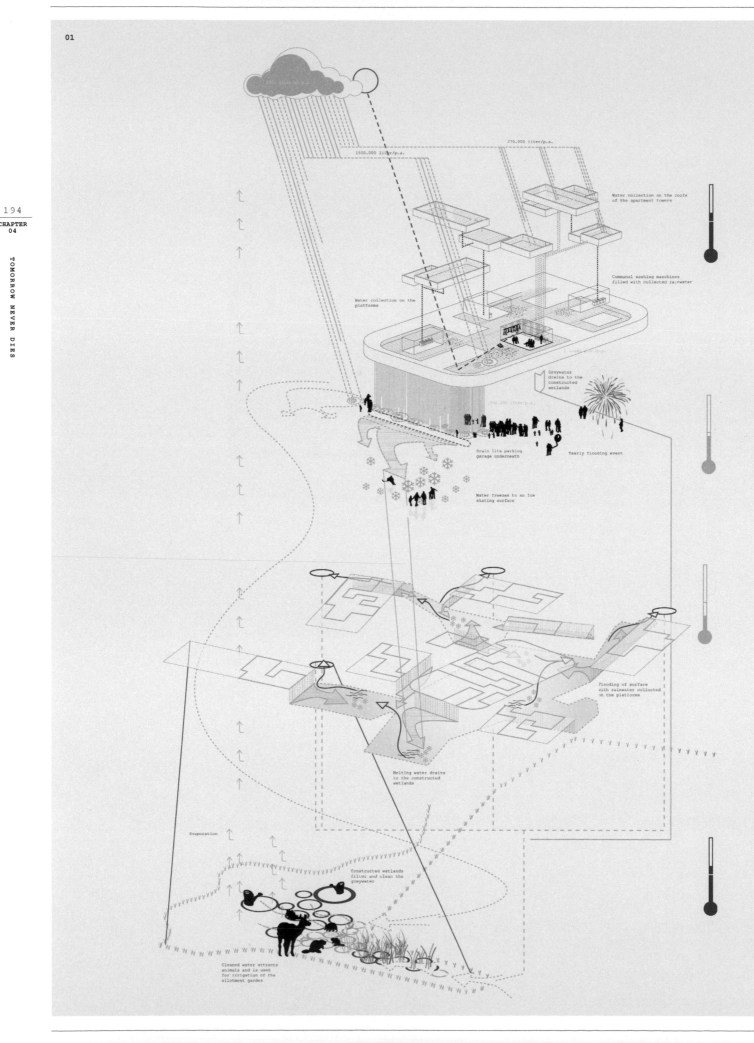

270.000 liter/p.a.

1500.000 liter/p.a.

Water collection on the roofs
of the apartment towers

Communal washing maschines
filled with collected rainwater

Water collection on the
platforms

Greywater
drains to the
constructed
wetlands

Drain lits parking
garage underneath

Yearly flooding event

Water freezes to an Ice
skating surface

Flooding of surface
with rainwater collected
on the platforms

Melting water drains
to the constructed
wetlands

Evaporation

Constructed wetlands
filter and clean the
greywater

Cleaned water attracts
animals and is used
for irrigation of the
allotment garden

02

01 Conceptual diagram.

02 Urban study models.

03 Inside Cumulus on a rainy day.

04 Public spaces in winter and summer.

03

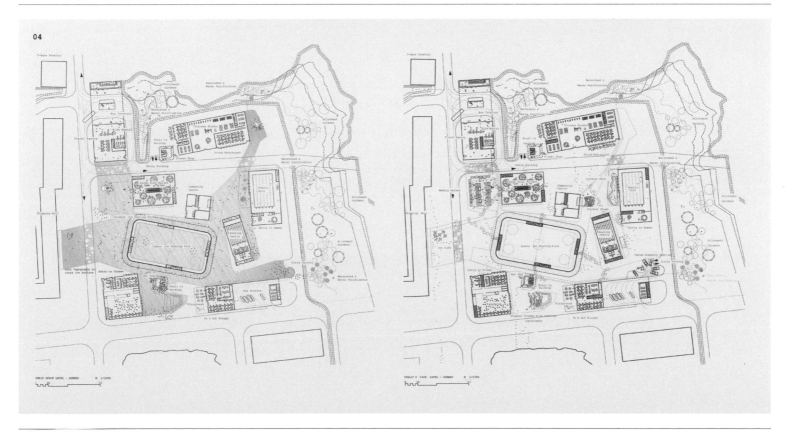

04

PEARCE ECOHOUSE
PETER JON PEARCE

ENGINEER
Pearce

CLIENT
Peter & Susan Pearce

PROJECT LOCATION
Malibu, USA

COMPLETION DATE
2011

01 Southern elevation. **02** Southeastern elevation. **03** Northern elevation. **04** Eastern elevation.

01 Property in the San-
   ta Monica Mountains
   showing minimum site
   intervention.

02/ Interior without
03 partitions, appli-
    ances, or furniture.

04 Shown without the
   supporting exoskele-
   ton, the enclosure
   envelope consists
   of 100 per cent in-
   sulated glass with
   operable windows in
   each vertical wall
   segment around the
   perimeter, and oper-
   able windows in the
   glass roof.

05 Elevation from the
   south showing adap-
   tation to site.

06 Roof plan comparing
   rendered image with
   louvers to grid of
   exoskeleton space-
   truss.

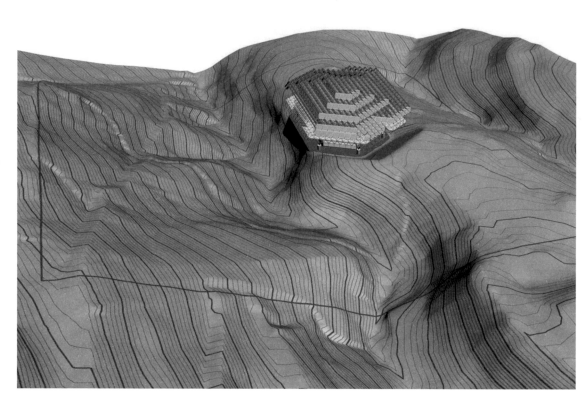

ASSIGNMENT

The aim of this prototypical private residence by product designer Peter Jon is to develop a high-performance design in which form, structure, process and materials are fully integrated to create a building that establishes the highest possible standards for sustainability and that demonstrates a design strategy based on readily available materials and manufacturing processes, unconstrained by conventional building methods and materials. ◣

LOCATION

The future construction site for the building is a 2.5-acre area with ocean views, at 670 metres elevation in the Santa Monica Mountains in the city of Malibu, California. This beachfront community on the Pacific coastline is famous for its warm and sandy beaches, and its proximity to the surrounding nature. ◣

CONCEPT

The concept of the Pearce Ecohouse is based on a high-performance design, ethics and strategy distinguished by Pearce's commitment to create products of exceptional performance, material efficiency, long life, and enduring appearance. Fundamental to the design is the development of a pre-engineered and pre-fabricated "kit-of-parts" from which the final building is assembled on site; the kit optimises engineering, structural, environmental, manufacturing, and installation performance. The goal of this undertaking is to provide a sense of well-being for the occupants through access to natural light, natural ventilation, environmental temperateness, sightlines to views, and adaptive open space. ◣

REALISATION

The Pearce Ecohouse comprises a building solution of low life-cycle cost. The residence is designed with an open span using a modular system of spatial subdivision enabling interior configurations to adapt to changing preferences. A high strength-to-weight structural system is used to support a building enclosure of low surface area to contained volume. The custom designed building components are manufactured from high-performance materials with high-recycled content such as steel, glass and synthetic stone. ◣

ENERGY CONCEPT

The Pearce Ecohouse is adapted to its site through optimum orientation and minimum site intervention with respect to topography, geology and native habitat. The building's ecological compatibility and energy efficiency are also seen in its zero energy use on an annualised basis. This is facilitated via grid-interactive photovoltaic collectors. A climate management canopy forms the architecture of the building. In so doing, solar radiation is managed in order to mitigate heat gain in the summer and collect heat in the winter. Operable windows provide natural ventilation, which is enhanced in hot weather through convection currents propelled by the climate management canopy. Thus, the building is solar cooled. Supplemental heating is provided by solar thermal collectors, which provide hot water for radiant floor heating and domestic hot water. Indirect natural light fills the glass enclosure, eliminating the need for artificial light during the day, with a concomitant savings in energy. Materials are selected for ease of manufacture, long life, low maintenance, and high recycled content. ◣

02

03

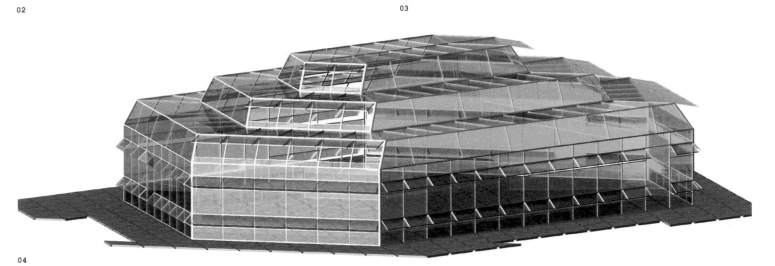

04

05

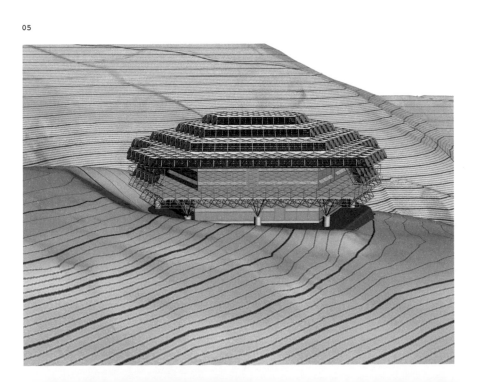

06

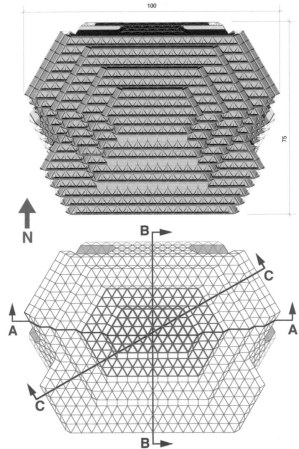

100

75

N

B

C

A   A

C

B

SUSTAINABLE HOUSING INITIATIVE: THE GINA STUDIO

STUDENTS FROM THE HARVARD GRADUATE SCHOOL OF DESIGN (WITH PROF. FRANK BARKOW AND PROF. CHRISTOPHER BANGLE)

CLIENT/SPONSOR
RMJM, Architects

PROJECT LOCATION
Various suburban sites, USA

COMPLETION DATE
2008

STUDENTS
Katy Barkan, Justin Chen, Anna Czigler, Ignacio Gonzalez Galan, Kent Gould, Meredith Harris, Stuart Helo, Daniel Hui, Jayne Kang, Vivien Liu, Payap (Gob) Pakdeelao, Megan Panzano, Joseph Ringenberg, Nora Yoo

01 Clustercity by Ingazio Gonzales Galan.

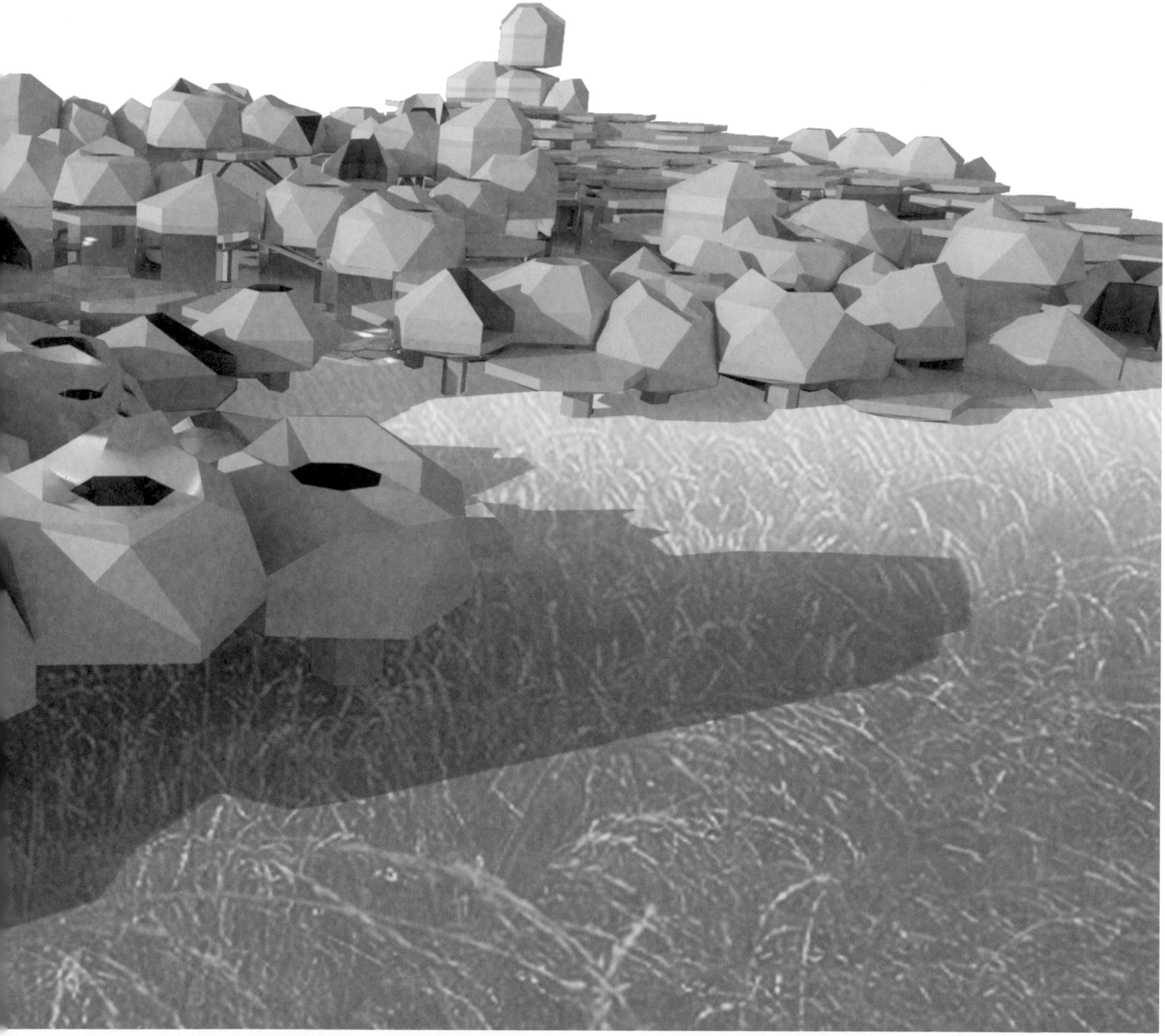

01
Clustercity by
Ingazio Gonzáles
Galán.

ASSIGNMENT

The goal of the studio was to appropriate an emerging technology, in the form of BMW's GINA Light Visionary concept car developed by Chris Bangle, and to understand how this might have a bearing on sustainable architecture for housing in the American suburb. The studio's work was situated in the context of rising fuel costs, the sub-prime mortgage home debacle, and the impulse for the suburb to become a place to work and live rather than a place from which to commute. GINA is particularly relevant to this purpose: it consists of a lightweight elastic skin that can move kinetically for both aesthetic/formal change or for performative/functional ones. The potential of this system for architecture is enormous. Surfaces, space-making, and programme can change in relationship to sustainability, economics of construction and transport. Students were asked to develop a prototypical house, understand its construction, materials, ability to be transported, and how it could aggregate and form a suburban community. They were also asked to consider the status of the car with respect to the house and how it should be integrated. ◣

CONCEPTS

The 14 students proposed a wide range of possibilities. Shown here are six selected projects:

Ignazio ("Nacho") Gonzáles Galán

This project began with the concept of an individual room that could cluster in multiples to form a single dwelling which could adapt and facilitate a full range of demographic and user types. The dwelling can multiply to create a carpet-like matrix of housing, allowing a density that would save open lands. The prefabricated cells would be placed on site-adjusted and specific concrete pads. The student developed an insulated fabric skin that worked like a fine mesh of apertures that could open or close, letting in light or air. This skin system is supported over a metal tube frame. This frame system can move and deform mechanically in order to enlarge a room spatially or to track sunlight (through an oculus) by opening or closing asymmetrically around the room floor plan. Dwellings can be enlarged or reduced by negotiating with neighbours. Empty cells create exterior terraces.

Kent Gould: The Teleburb

The Teleburb uses a telescoping principle to expand or contract the living programme seasonally while allowing the housing to act infrastructurally, adjusting itself to roadways or to volatile (problematic) sites. This means arid sites, or sites prone to flooding, could be negotiated by clusters of Teleburb housing, which creates armatures that can telescope but also rise up or down along central spine-hubs. The ends of these armatures extend to roadways where cars can drive into the individual homes. The structure of the Teleburb consists of pre-manufactured segments constructed like aircraft sections which have a mesh-like skin that can adjust to light and weather conditions. One of the more utopian proposals, the Teleburb is intended to colonise leftover problematic sites damaged by flooding, aridity, brownfield sites, or those damaged by mining or military uses.

Justin Chen: Cloud Suburbia

Justin Chen's project also uses a cellular system of room organisation with tent-like volumes that deform along a tracking system to change spatially and directionally along a deformed organisational grid. Chen used grasshopper-scripting software to conceive, imagine and construct a range of scenarios. The transformative ability of his project can change rooms, doors and windows for each living space. The Cloud Suburbia is situated over

ENERGY CONCEPT

The overriding principle was one of ephemerality - that is, after Buckminster Fuller, the use of lightweight materials that are cheaper to manufacture, use fewer resources, and are easier to transport and install. In most cases, fabric is in these projects a material that is used kinetically: this means sustainability, controlling light, sun shading, weather, insulation, ventilation, and space can be achieved by moving surfaces. The dream of kinetic architecture is realised with these projects where both formal and aesthetic desires are mediated by performative and functional results - an interesting proposition when housing costs, fuel costs, and the status of the car, identity, and sense of place demand a re-thinking of the American suburb. ◣

the air-right spaces of freeway infrastructure in Orange County, California. Cars can off-ramp into communal elevators, which lift them to a large bridge structure that accommodates the suburban community. Additional density is achieved with the addition of commercial/work towers near the matt housing structure. The Cloud Suburbia would then integrate into existing adjacent suburban neighbourhoods.

Vivien Liu

This project operates at the scale of infrastructure: it is like a lattice or scaffolding that can adapt, change or react to an existing in-fill. Viviane Liu looked at case studies like the Free University of Berlin from Team 10 as a way to understand how a residential carpet scheme could function. Another reference for her work are the ornamental screen walls from Hauer from the 1950s. The superstructure is conceived as a framework of pre-cast concrete. This matrix of mass-customised, digitally formed concrete is colonised by infilling the frames with elastic (non-bearing) fabric partition walls that define and enclose individual living units. These units can expand or contract as negotiated with neighbours similar to other projects. The fabric shells have the ability to slide on tracks like a convertible car to open the living units to the sky. Cars are parked on the lower superstructure levels in close proximity to the apartments.

Daniel Hui: Flat Pack

This project considers a very low-cost and compact rectangular container, which is articulated as a series of redundant, mass-customised glulaminated wood frames. Within these frames, a series of fabric gaskets or louvers move and adapt to modulate lighting conditions locally and along the length of the building. While the frames are fixed, the louvers change and can be monitored digitally. The frame sizes are calculated to mediate costs and for ease of transport and easy erecting on site. The interior spaces of the house are carved out to provide a variable living programme. The interstitial depth of the frame is structural but is also given over to storage spaces for the project. A car can drive into the space on the end, and the houses can multiply and be arranged to create a community of like structures. ◣

01

02

03

04

01 Rendering of stacked dwelling by Megan Panzano.   **02** Interior rendering of Flat Pack by Daniel Hui.   **03** Teleburb in arid location.   **04** Teleburb by Kent Gould. Location prone to flooding.

The "wind dam", a giant swath of
fabric connected to a turbine,
looks more like a Christo art
installation than a power
generator.

CHAPTER
04

TOMORROW NEVER DIES

ENGINEER
WSP Finlan

CLIENT
Confidential

PROJECT LOCATION
Lake Ladoga, Russia

COMPLETION DATE
Ongoing

WIND DAM
LAURIE CHETWOOD

01 The dam pictured over a gorge at Lake Ladoga in northwest Russia.

02 / Boosting productivity
03 by capturing high-speed-winds with a massive spinnaker sail.

ASSIGNMENT

The brief from the client was straightforward: research and find the most efficient way of harnessing wind power. Wind power is one of the fastest growing forms of energy production worldwide. There is a great deal of international interest in research, and many governments are planning and implementing the installation of huge wind farms with acres of turbines. A problem with wind turbines, however, is that they are usually not very effective at catching the wind; more wind tends to flow around them than pass through the rotor blades. Another problem is that they are not particularly beautiful en masse and have a large visual impact on the environments where they are installed. ◤

LOCATION

The first wind dam is planned to be suspended across the mouth of a fjord-like gorge opening into Lake Ladoga, in northwest Russia 40 kilometres from St. Petersburg. It is the largest lake in Europe. ◤

REALISATION

The wind dam has yet to be built. It will be tethered between two land masses strategically located to harness the prevailing wind. The funnelling effect of a gorge or narrow valley will concentrate the mass of air captured by the sail and is divert it through a turbine, generating electricity. Simulation, wind tunnel testing and vibration analysis are currently being carried out for a number of locations in Russia. WSP Finland's wind engineering director, Risto Kiviluoma, has provided technical support and advice for a project that has never been attempted on this scale before: "There will be many technical challenges to solve: the type of turbine to use, the construction method, structural design and safety in major storms." ◤

ENERGY CONCEPT

With a sail height of 25 metres, a width of 75 metres, and three 15 to 20kM turbines placed one behind the other to capture as much of the wind energy as possible, and an average wind speed of ten metres per second, the predicted annual energy output is between 100 and 120 megawatts per year. That would meet the energy requirements of 28 to 35 houses per year, based on average UK housing requirements of 3500 kilowatts per annum. ◤

CONCEPT

Surely there must be other, more efficient and more aesthetic ways of harnessing wind energy. British architect Laurie Chetwood is working together with the structural engineering firm WSP Finland to develop a wind dam capable of harnessing relatively minimal wind volumes at low speeds. This would generate power via a turbine more efficiently than by current means. The dam, which would be located over a gorge at Lake Ladoga in northwest Russia, includes a cup-shaped spinnaker sail, which will generate renewable energy by funnelling the wind through an attached turbine. The spinnaker shape is similar to the mainsail of a yacht and is thought to be particularly effective in capturing wind which should then be funnelled smoothly and steadily through the turbine to generate power. The shape of the sail was influenced because of its functionality and the desire to produce something sculptural, says Chetwood: "The sail looks like a bird dipping its beak into the water, which will be much less of a blot on this beautiful and unblemished landscape." But it is also highly effective at capturing the wind because it replicates the work of a dam and does not let the wind escape in the way that occurs with traditional propellers. Instead, it funnels it like a giant wind sock. ◤

01 Elevation of Nano Vent-Skin on fictional tower building. The outer skin of the structure absorbs sunlight through an organic photovoltaic layer and transforms it into energy in the nano-fibres inside the nano-wires. The energy is subsequently sent to the storage units at the end of each panel.

02 The Nano Vent-skin uses micro-organisms combined with mechanics to make existing objects greener by giving them a skin made of micro wind turbines.

NANO VENT-SKIN
AGUSTIN OTEGUI

CLIENT
Personal project

PROJECT LOCATION
Concept

COMPLETION DATE
Ongoing

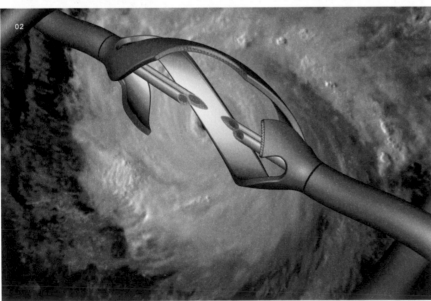

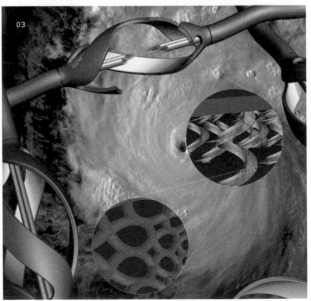

01/02/03
Structural detail. The thousands of micro turbines embedded in the fabric of the
skin generate energy from wind and sunlight. They also absorb CO2 and produce oxygen.

04
Elevation of Nano-Vent
Skin tower on sandy shore.

ASSIGNMENT

Nano Vent-Skin (NVS) is a personal research concept by the Mexican/Spanish product designer Agustin Otegui aimed at triggering new approaches towards greener, more energy-efficient structures. "This project was born after seeing all the gigantic projects being built around the world where it seems that in order to be green you have to think big and build something impressively huge," says Otegui. "Why don't we start thinking on a smaller scale so we can use existing structures to generate energy?" ◤

CONCEPT

The main purpose of the Nano Vent-Skin concept was to develop an alternative method of absorbing and generating clean energy. The intention was also to demonstrate to other specialists in this field the possibility of generating energy on a smaller scale and applying it to existing buildings, houses and structures such as tunnels, road barriers, etc., to generate energy. The Nano Vent-Skin uses micro-organisms combined with mechanics to make existing objects greener by giving them a skin made of micro wind turbines. The thousands of micro turbines embedded in the fabric of the skin, each 25 mm x 10.8 mm in size, generate energy from wind and sunlight; they also absorb CO_2 and produced oxygen. Finally, the product is made from 100 per cent recyclable materials.

NVS is based on nanotechnology – a controversial research area that is nevertheless playing an increasing role in technological developments and may soon become a common method of manufacture for everyday products, says Otegui: "Nowadays controversy runs around the topic of scientists playing God in trying to reshape organisms and living things. It's true that we run the risk of not knowing what the consequences will be. But we have to think as well of all the benefits we are missing out on. Nature is a 4.5-billion-year-old research centre of trial and error. The more we learn and take advantage of this huge database, the less we run into dead-end solutions. We can't improve nature. It does this by itself and in ways we will never achieve. It even reinvents itself in order to survive in areas where humankind is trying to destroy it. NVS is not attempting to reinvent or reshape nature either. It's just acting as a merger of different means and approaches in energy absorption and transformation, which would never happen in nature. For example: a palm tree can never learn from an arctic raspberry bush or a bonsai tree if they never coexist within the same surroundings." NVS takes advantage of globalised knowledge of different species and resources and turns them into a joint organism where three different ways of absorbing and transforming energy work in symbiosis. Using nano-manufacturing with bioengineered organisms as a production method, NVS merges different kinds of micro-organisms that work together to absorb and transform natural energy from the environment. What comes out of this merging of living organisms is a skin that transforms two of the most abundant sources of green energy on earth: sunlight and wind. ◤

ENERGY CONCEPT

The outer skin of the NVS structure absorbs sunlight through an organic photovoltaic layer and transforms it into energy in the nano-fibres inside the nano-wires; the energy is subsequently sent to the storage units at the end of each panel. Each turbine on the panel generates energy via chemical reactions at each end where it makes contact with the structure. Polarised micro-organisms are responsible for this process on every turbine's turn. The inner skin of each turbine works as a filter absorbing CO_2 from the environment as wind passes through it. Each panel has four supply units. These units monitor that all the turbines are working and deliver material to regenerate broken or malfunctioning turbines. They also receive and store the energy produced by the turbines. The goal in using nano-bioengineering and nano-manufacturing as a means of production is to achieve an efficient zero-emission material which uses the right kind and amount of material where needed. These micro-organisms have not been genetically altered; they work as a trained colony where each member has a specific task in this symbiotic process. Every panel has a sensor on each corner with a material reservoir. When one of the turbines has a failure or breaks, a signal is sent through the nano-wires to the central system and building material (micro-organisms) are sent through the central tube to regenerate this area with a self-assembly process. In order to achieve the best outcome of energy, the blades of each turbine are symmetrically designed; even if the wind direction changes, each turbine can adapt by rotating either clockwise or anti-clockwise, depending on the situation. ◤

NORTH
TERRITORIAL AGENCY
(JOHN PALMESINO, ANN-SOFI RÖNNSKOG)

CLIENT
Slought Foundation

PROJECT LOCATION
The Arctic and Subarctic
Territories

COMPLETION DATE
2007–2008

01 Relief of North Pole. The
    inhabited territories at the
    northern latitudes are facing
    unprecedented changes.

02 Vector drawing of North Pole.

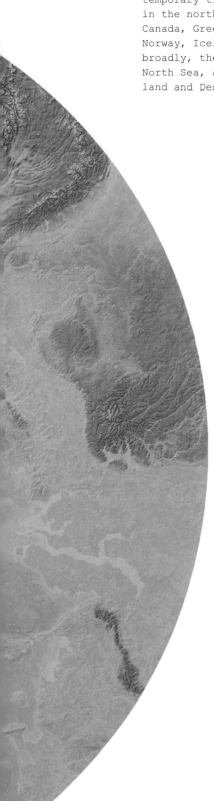

ASSIGNMENT

Climate change is not the only transformation we are facing today in the North.

LOCATION

"North" is a spatial analysis of the unfolding contemporary transformations in the north of the U.S., Canada, Greenland, Russia, Norway, Iceland, and, more broadly, the UK with the North Sea, and Sweden, Finland and Denmark. ◢

The North is slowlyrevealing a system of transformations in the physical, institutional, social, spatial, economic and cultural structures we inhabit and constantly reshape. Today, transformations in the relationship between polities and space are stressed in the northern latitudes more than anywhere else on the globe. At the same time as this region is undergoing unprecedented changes, our vision of it is entrenched in stereotypical notions of pure and untouched wilderness, unfolding and innocent modernity and untamed mineral and biological resources. The urgent questions that the inhabitation, crossing and exploitation of the North pose demand new tools and a reinvention of our way of thinking and articulating the relationship between the material configuration of human environments and the forms of our societies and institutions. ◢

CONCEPT

An analysis of this kind can reveal a set of links and unexpected relationships that a sectorial investigation might overlook. Architecture might be used as an inquiry method, as a probe into the unstable links between the form of our local, national and international polities, and their space of operation. By analysing the spatial articulations of the current race to ensure access to natural resources and at the same time evaluate the consequences of climate change, the research departed from the current debates in international law and aggregate visions. It did this to consider the intricate relations and multidimensional connections between the form of inhabited environment and the contemporary polities beyond national and international agencies. Territorial Agency works towards the development of a complex representation of the interrelations between these sectorial and expert rationalities. With the development of a multidimensional critical cartography, it represents transformations that are marking the transition of the northern regions away from their apparently immaculate standstill, towards a rapidly shifting space of cultural and geopolitical engagement. Territorial Agency devised the project entitled "North" as an occasion to think about how water is rapidly becoming the central issue in the management of inhabited territories. The changing conditions related to its ownership, protection from shortages and excesses, disputes over sovereignty, as well as underwater oil and mineral resource exploitation, are modifying our perception of the geography of large parts of the northern European regions, of the Arctic Sea and North America. This research project addresses these themes by investigating a number of case studies, from the oil resources off the coasts of Norway, to the disputed continental shelf under the North Pole, to the waterway access of Russia on the Baltic. By shifting our understanding of location away from nation states and towards geographical regions and the interplay of different fields, "North" explores the dynamic relationships between contemporary politics and their spaces of operation. ◢

02

REALISATION

The project was initiated by Territorial Agency in 2007 and then further developed as part of the RBSL Bergman Foundation Curatorial Seminar at the University of Pennsylvania, taught by Professor Aaron Levy and the Slought Foundation in Philadelphia. Throughout the 2007-2008 academic year, students in the course collaboratively undertook research in conjunction with Territorial Agency architects John Palmesino and Ann-Sofi Rönnskog, collecting and constructing a series of archives and materials representative of the various forces and fields of influence currently operating in the conflict-ridden Northern Territories. In the process, the students engaged in research spanning disciplines such as literature, geo-political studies, visual culture, architecture, and urbanism, as well as science and technology. The students collaborated and interacted with Territorial Agency through a variety of modes of communication ranging from personal interaction to video conferencing. The result was a display in the vault galleries at Slought Foundation and a public event featuring the collaborative research undertaken by Territorial Agency and the seminar students. ◢

ZEEKRACHT
OFFICE FOR METROPOLITAN ARCHITECTURE

CLIENT
Natuur en Milieu

PROJECT LOCATION
North Sea, Netherlands

COMPLETION DATE
TBD, current phase is
a strategic masterplan
extending to 2040

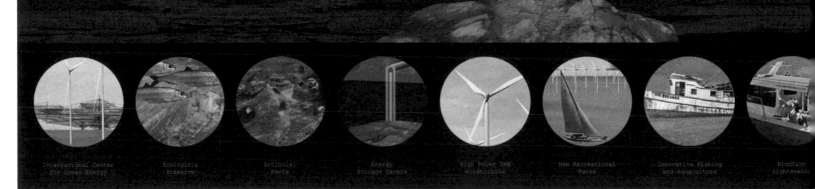

International Center
for Ocean Energy

Ecobicycle
Preserve

Artificial
Reefs

Energy
Storage Cavern

High Power 5MW
Windturbine

New Recreational
Parks

Innovative Fishing
and Aquaculture

Windfarm
Sightseeing

01 Collage of the development of the North Sea as a sustainable energy source.

Small Gas
Cavern

Decommissioned
Oil Rig

Ecotourium

Diving and
Wildlife Watching

Historic
Shipwreck

Energy
Super-Ring

Marine
Recreation

Dutch
Town

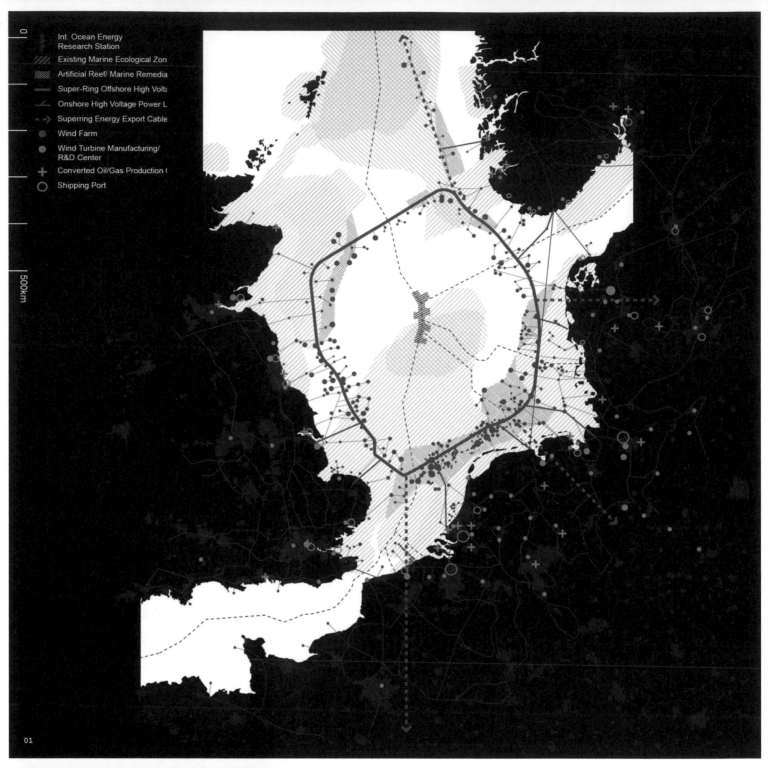

Int. Ocean Energy
Research Station

Existing Marine Ecological Zon

Artificial Reef/ Marine Remedia

Super-Ring Offshore High Volt

Onshore High Voltage Power L

Superring Energy Export Cable

Wind Farm

Wind Turbine Manufacturing/
R&D Center

Converted Oil/Gas Production (

Shipping Port

0

500km

01

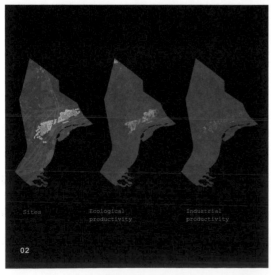

Sites

Ecological
productivity

Industrial
productivity

02

01 The North Sea
masterplan is
envisioned as the
natural result
of international
cooperative off-
shore development.
Rather then a fixed
plan, it propo-
ses a system of
catalytic elements
that if envisioned
in the present
could optimise the
use of the sea in
the future.

02 Farms develop along
ecological zones
and around existing
decommissioned
platforms, creating
marine remediati-
on areas, recrea-
tional parks, and
recreational sea
routes. At a mature
stage of offshore
development, wind
farms are clustered
along the length of
a Super Ring, sup-
plying and tapping
the supranational
supply efficiently.

03 North Sea
Masterplan
areal site
with connect-
ing countries.

04 Primary compo-
nents of the North
Sea Masterplan.
From above left to
bottom right: the
Energy Super Ring,
the Production
Belt, the Reefs
and the Interna-
tional Research
Centre.

LOCATION

The North Sea, 970 kilometres by 580 kilometres, is bordered by the Orkney Islands, England Scotland, Denmark, Norway, Sweden, Germany, The Netherlands, Belgium and France. It contains some of the world's busiest and important trade routes and has a total area of 750.000 square kilometres. ◣

and the International Research Centre - promoting international cooperation, research, innovation and development. The North Sea Masterplan proposes an operative development strategy for immediate national implementation that simultaneously takes into account long-term development and coordination of national and supra-national interests. Unlike the usual technocratic planning methods based on least-conflict zoning, the masterplan suggests a proactive and multi-dimensional approach based on enabling possibility. The proposed circular wind farms provide destinations at sea through their explicit connection with the parties they are supplying (e.g. communities, companies, cities, etc.). The farms are also designed to be situated, programmed and phased according to the evolving demands and plans of North Sea regional development. Locally, the wind farms perform a series of hybrid functions according to their location and performance mandate - depleted underwater natural gas reservoirs are used for energy storage, untapped gas fields for hybrid energy production, farms adjacent to shipping lanes act as offshore power stations, etc. Farms developed along ecological zones and around existing decommissioned platforms create marine remediation areas, new recreational parks, and recreational sea routes. At a mature stage of offshore development, wind farms are clustered along the length of the Super Ring, distributing national surpluses and supplying regional energy needs efficiently and profitably. The masterplan is a strategic blueprint comprised of wind farms that perform on multiple levels, new destinations and new programmes at sea, maximising the industrial and eco productivity of the North Sea area. ◣

ASSIGNMENT

Natuur en Milieu (The Netherlands Society for Nature and the Environment) has set a goal for the Netherlands to play a leading role in the development of a sustainable future. To achieve this goal, Natuur en Milieu developed the North Sea Masterplan, which proposes placing giant wind farms in the North Sea with a capacity of 8000 mega watts - enough to provide for the annual electricity needs of all Dutch households. Natuur en Milieu approached the Office for Metropolitan Architecture (OMA*AMO) with the request to develop a masterplan for the North Sea as a sustainable energy source. This masterplan will form a new and realistic vision for the future of the North Sea, taking into account present and future claims and opportunities, national and supranational perspectives. The masterplan will investigate how wind energy and its required infrastructure can stimulate international cooperation and communication on ecological, political and industrial levels. ◣

CONCEPT/ENERGY CONCEPT

Due to its high and consistent wind speeds, shallow waters, dense population and knowledge industry, the North Sea is arguably the most suitable area for large-scale wind farms in the world. The potential magnitude for renewable energy in the North Sea, say the architects, approaches that of fossil fuel production in the Persian Gulf states today. In the changing landscape of twenty-first-century energy perception and demand, the North Sea could become a major player in global energy production and trade through wind power alone. The North Sea Masterplan is envisioned as the result of cooperative international offshore development. Rather than a fixed spatial plan, it proposes a system of catalytic elements that, while envisioned for the present, are optimised for long-term sustainability. Primary components of the North Sea Masterplan include the Energy Super Ring - the primary infrastructure for energy distribution and supply; the Production Belt - the industrial and institutional infrastructure supporting research and manufacturing; the Reefs - stimulated marine ecologies reinforcing the natural eco-systems (and eco-productivity) of the sea;

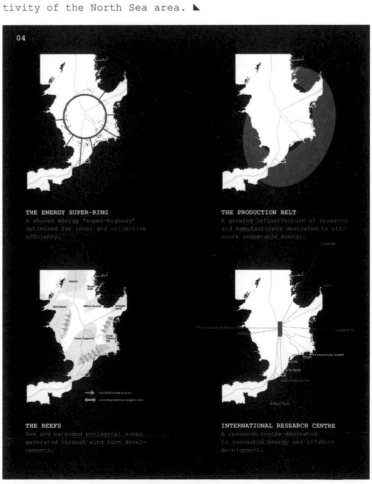

THE ENERGY SUPER-RING
A shared energy 'super-highway' optimised for local and collective efficiency.

THE PRODUCTION BELT
A growing infrastructure of research and manufacturers dedicated to offshore renew-able energy.

THE REEFS
New and extended ecological zones generated through wind farm developments.

INTERNATIONAL RESEARCH CENTRE
A research centre dedicated to renewable energy and offshore development.

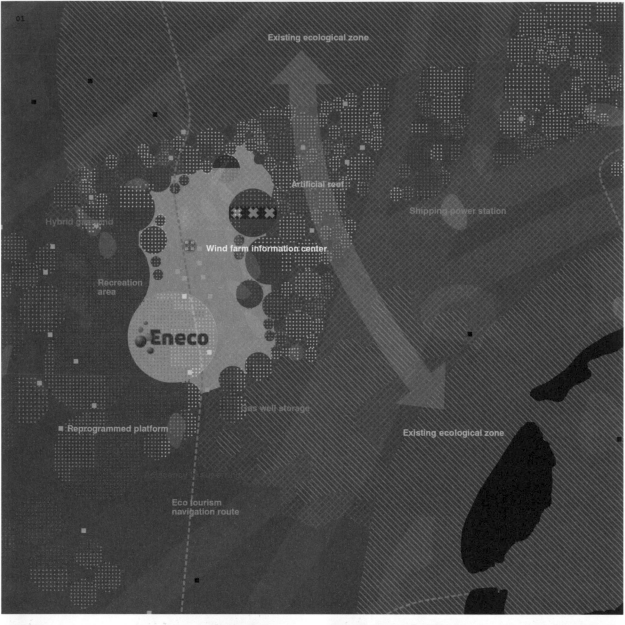

Existing ecological zone

Artificial reef

Shipping power station

Hybrid gas wind

Wind farm information center

Recreation
area

Eneco

Gas well storage

Reprogrammed platform

Existing ecological zone

Adjacency to superring

Eco tourism
navigation route

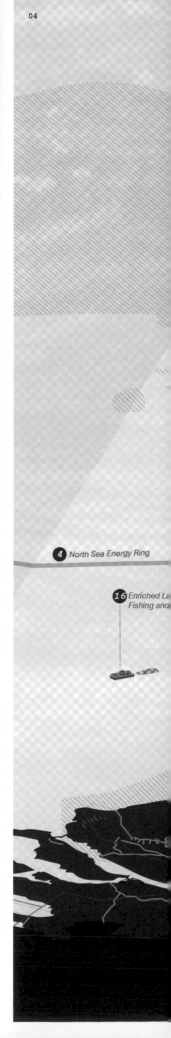

4 North Sea Energy Ring

16 Enriched La
Fishing and

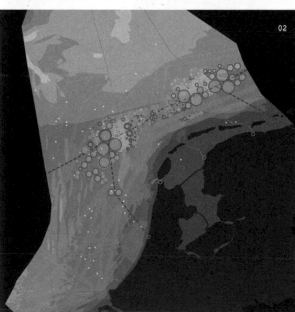

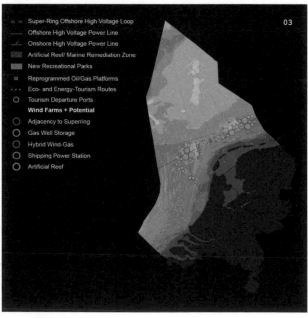

- Super-Ring Offshore High Voltage Loop
- Offshore High Voltage Power Line
- Onshore High Voltage Power Line
- Artificial Reef/ Marine Remediation Zone
- New Recreational Parks
- Reprogrammed Oil/Gas Platforms
- Eco- and Energy-Tourism Routes
- Tourism Departure Ports
- **Wind Farms + Potential**
- Adjacency to Superring
- Gas Well Storage
- Hybrid Wind-Gas
- Shipping Power Station
- Artificial Reef

01 Defining the development: by creating
circular plots for wind-farm developments, a series of sites is created.

02/ Strategic national planning methods
03 are proposed to secure the collective
potentials of the sea and its use in
the future. A proactive and multi-dimensional approach based on possibility seems feasible.

04 The North Sea Masterplan proposes
an integrated system connecting the
local user to international policy
through common interests and shared
goals.

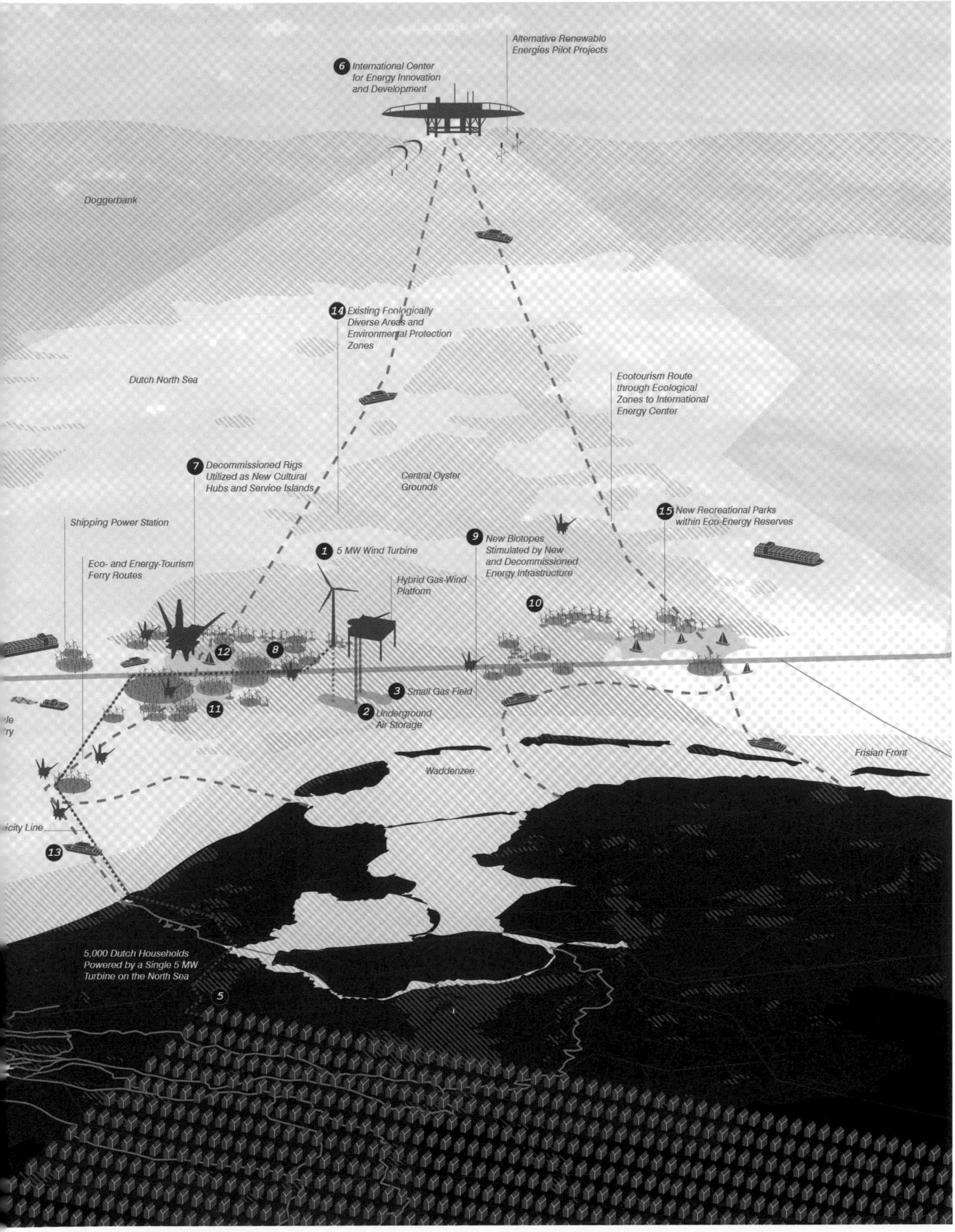

6 International Center for Energy Innovation and Development

Alternative Renewable Energies Pilot Projects

Doggerbank

14 Existing Ecologically Diverse Areas and Environmental Protection Zones

Dutch North Sea

Ecotourism Route through Ecological Zones to International Energy Center

7 Decommissioned Rigs Utilized as New Cultural Hubs and Service Islands

Central Oyster Grounds

15 New Recreational Parks within Eco-Energy Reserves

Shipping Power Station

9 New Biotopes Stimulated by New and Decommissioned Energy Infrastructure

Eco- and Energy-Tourism Ferry Routes

1 5 MW Wind Turbine

Hybrid Gas-Wind Platform

10

12   **8**

11

3 Small Gas Field

2 Underground Air Storage

Waddenzee

Frisian Front

le
ry

icity Line

13

5.000 Dutch Households Powered by a Single 5 MW Turbine on the North Sea

5

SELF-SUFFICIENT CITY
TERREFUGE

CLIENT
City of New York

PROJECT LOCATION
New York, NY, USA

COMPLETION DATE
Ongoing research

01

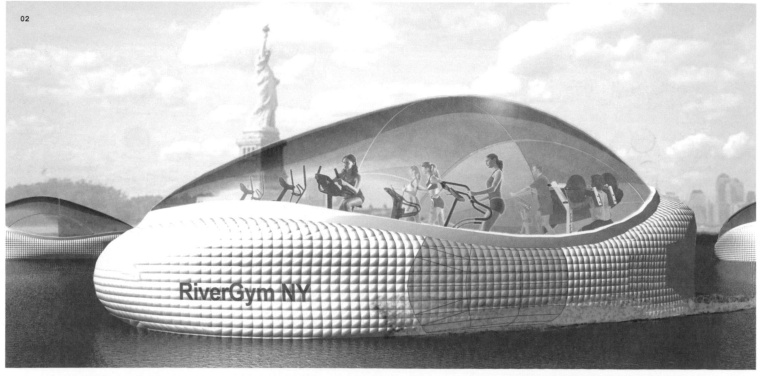

02

01 Transporation systems for a new vision of the city.

02 Human powered river gyms that travel in 15 minute loops.

03 Blimp-Bumper Bus scoop passengers up on the fly in soft chairs.

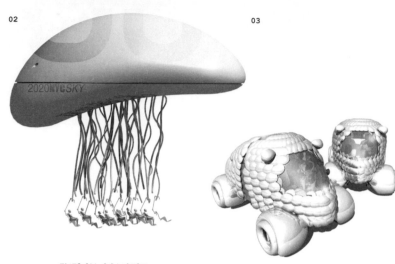

TOMORROW NEVER DIES

ASSIGNMENT

This research project by Terrefuge is for the sustainable future of New York. It is a conceptual master plan based on the premise that rapid growth, rising sea levels, urban heat island effect, and massive climate change will fundamentally alter the city. New York City is envisioned as existing in a fully autonomous and self-sufficient state without any inputs or outputs from its borders. Key areas of investigation include waste, water, food, mobility, energy and habitat. The experiment investigates precisely how far the city can reasonably go in taking care of these needs within its political borders. The Self-Sufficient City concept is predicated on testing the limits of New York's physical capacity to take political responsibility for its own respiratory requirements within 100 years. ◣

LOCATION

The entire city of New York on the East Coast of the United States. Historical home to waves of immigration, this place was chosen by Terrefuge for its history of social and architectural transformation. ◣

CONCEPT

This project is about thinking on a colossal scale; urban infrastructure and urban resources will forever massively change to benefit the life of the planet. The project seeks to balance boundaries – the borders of New York City – that are largely arbitrary from an environmental point of view but decisive from a political one. It is, in effect, a plan for testing the limits of the city's capacity to become self-sufficient in a range of areas that are vital to its survival and to its relationship to the sustainability of the planet as a whole. To do this, the research applies the economic model of import substitution, not simply to the production of goods and services but to the environmental performance of the city more generally conceived. ◣

REALISATION

New York City can lead the way by reducing its footprint on its own geography. Key measures include harvesting energy from the sun and wind, greening the city

01-03
Blimp Bumper Bus, a low-floating air lift and Car Lambs using low pressure soy-based pillows as body.

to cool it down, collecting rainwater, bio-remediating wastes for inhabitation, growing large amounts of food, softening vehicles and taking back streets for pedestrians. New York should profoundly consider the following agendas: technologically advanced vehicles, re-imagining work on the basis of the continuous replacement of imports, remaking neighbourhoods to provide all of the needs of daily life within walking distance of home, abandoning zoning by use in favour of allowing multi-use areas, recycling old buildings into new ones, and thinking about every single aspect of planning in design with the goal of maximising independence. Terrefuge proposes a transformation of the city via a radical strategy: the reversal of figure and ground, of public and private property. Beginning with citywide greenfill, the immediate transfer of half the aggregate of street space from the vehicular to the pedestrian and public realm. Later, the streets become building sites and, as new, highly autonomous, buildings grow in intersections and wind their way down streets and avenues and through vacant lots, the old, deteriorated fabric will fade away to be replaced both by an abundance of productive green space and by a new labyrinth of irregular blocks, a paradise for people on foot. Fast movement will be accomplished underground in a superbly modernised subway and along the rivers and new cross-island channels. The city streets – extended in their length but reduced in their area – will support a marvellous technology we know to be just over the horizon, some fabulous and slow conveyance summoned with a whistle or collapsed into a pocket. ◣

ENERGY CONCEPT

One of Terrefuge's thought experiments is to reduce global energy consumption by reusing waste materials. A landfill such as Fresh Kills on New York's Staten Island is an easy mine for a future city. The city is disposing of 36,200 tonnes of waste per day. Most of this discarded material ended up in Fresh Kills landfill before it closed. The Self-Sufficient City plan supposes an extended New York reconstituted from its own landfill material. Terrefuge's concept remakes the city by using the trash at Fresh Kills. With this method, seven entirely new Manhattan islands can be remade at full scale. Automated, robotic three-dimensional printers are modified to process trash and complete this task within decades. These robots are based on existing off-the-self techniques commonly found in industrial waste compaction devices. Instead of machines that crush objects into cubes, these devices have jaws that make simple puzzle blocks for assembly. Different materials serve specified purposes: plastic for fenestration, organic compounds for temporary scaffolds, metals for primary structures, etc. Eventually, the future city makes no distinction between waste and supply. Another massive energy concept for this city revolves around the sun. Terrefuge estimated that an area the size of Queens covered with photovoltaics at 15 per cent efficiency will be enough to power the city per year. The cost is roughly four times that of current non-renewable power technologies and sources. Terrefuge uses these data to produce many needed iterations of New York City as an independent energy island. The idea is to later integrate different strategies to make clean renewable energy affordable, infinite and realisable within 50 years. ◣

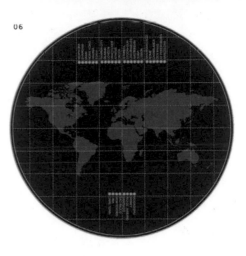

04 Temperature increases
as North Pole melts.

05 Desirable real estate
will be in the north.

06 World cities drift to
the poles.

07 World cities converge
to form a new Pangea.

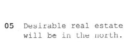

01 Elevation of the Self-Sufficient City. Population is
capped at nine million. No
inputs, no outputs within
NYC political boundaries.

02 Every hour, New York produces enough waste to fill the
Statue of Liberty.

03 Existing Lower East Side.

04 New concept plan.

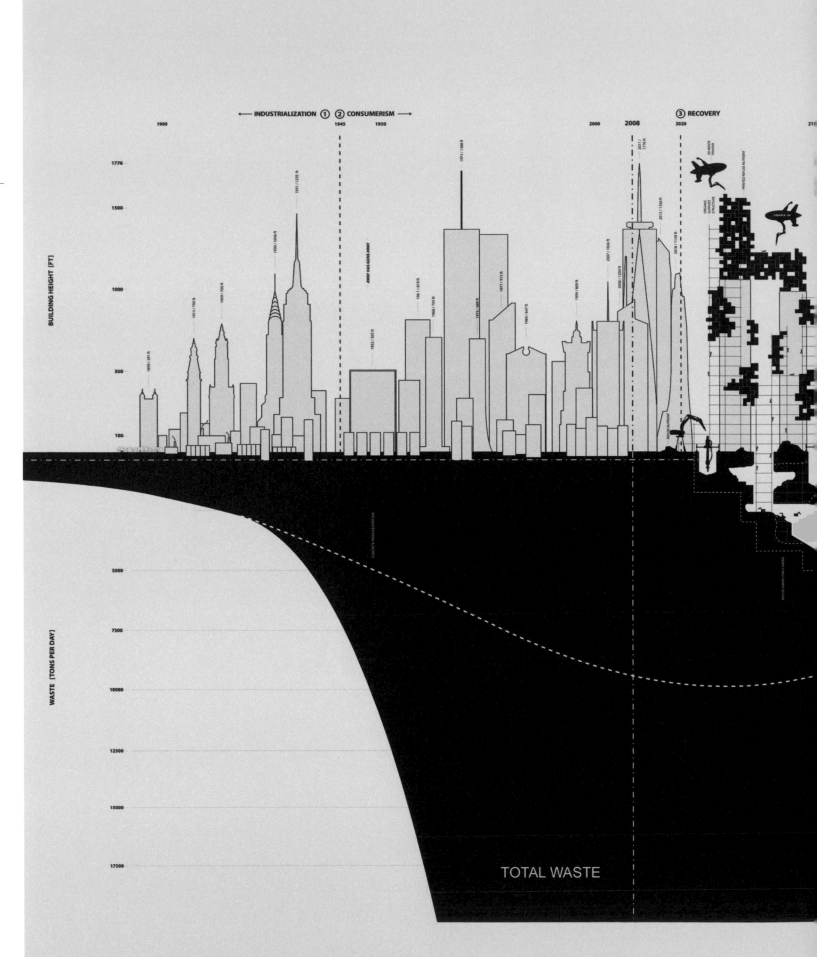

01 History and future of garbage.

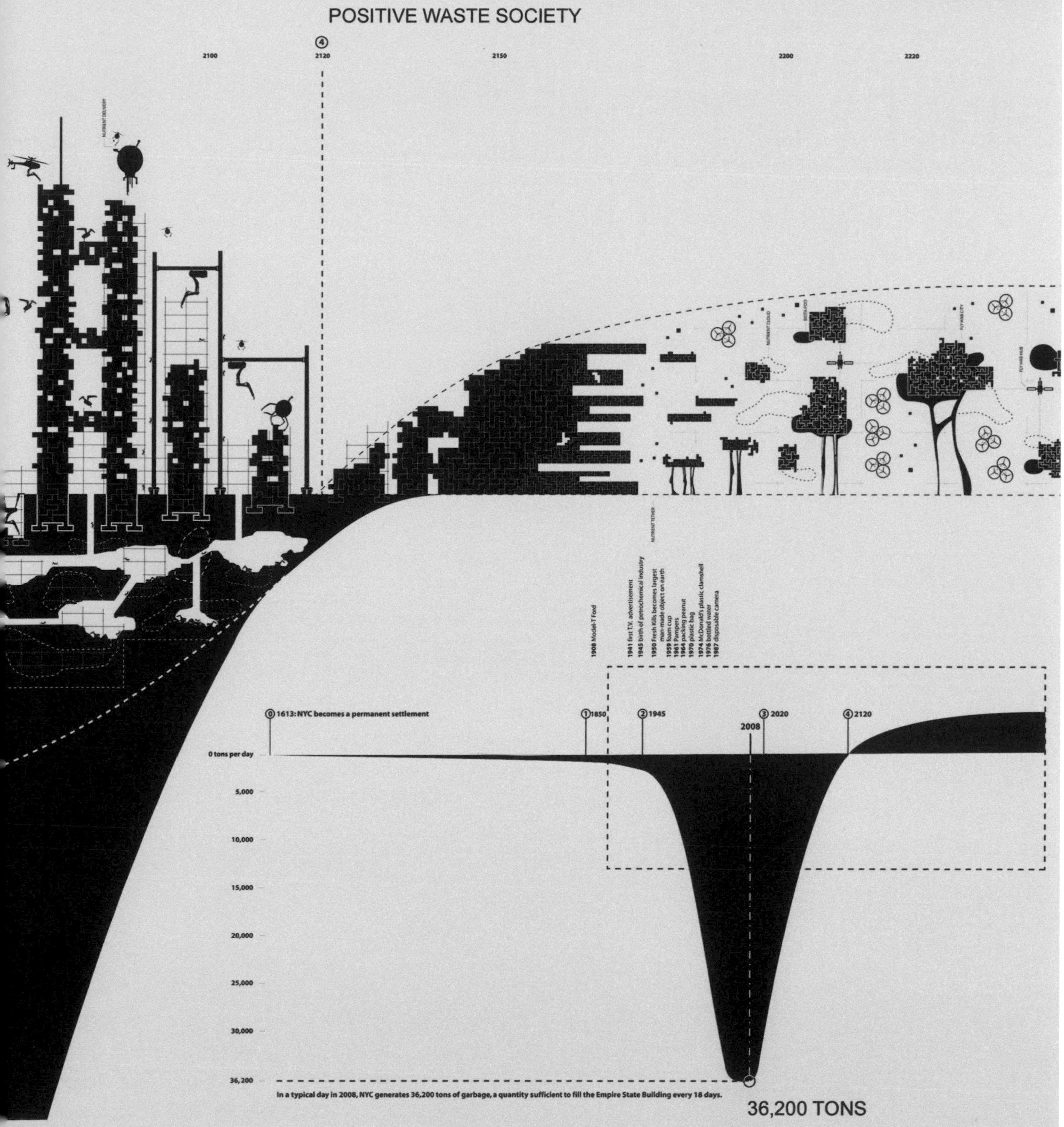
POSITIVE WASTE SOCIETY
4
2100
2120
2150
2200
2220
NUTRIENT DELIVERY
NUTRIENT CLOUD
BIOTA POD
FLY HAB CITY
FLY HAB HUB
NUTRIENT TETHER
1908 Model-T Ford
1941 first T.V. advertisement
1945 birth of petrochemical industry
1950 Fresh Kills becomes largest man-made object on earth
1959 foam cup
1961 Pampers
1964 packing peanut
1970 plastic bag
1974 McDonald's plastic clamshell
1976 bottled water
1987 disposable camera
0 1613: NYC becomes a permanent settlement
1 1850
2 1945
3 2020
4 2120
2008
0 tons per day
5,000
10,000
15,000
20,000
25,000
30,000
36,200
In a typical day in 2008, NYC generates 36,200 tons of garbage, a quantity sufficient to fill the Empire State Building every 18 days.
36,200 TONS

GREEN DESERT MINE
CHRISTOPHE DM BARLIEB ARCHITECTS

ENGINEER
Schlaich Bergermann Solar

PROJECT LOCATION
Eastern Sahara

COMPLETION DATE
Ongoing research

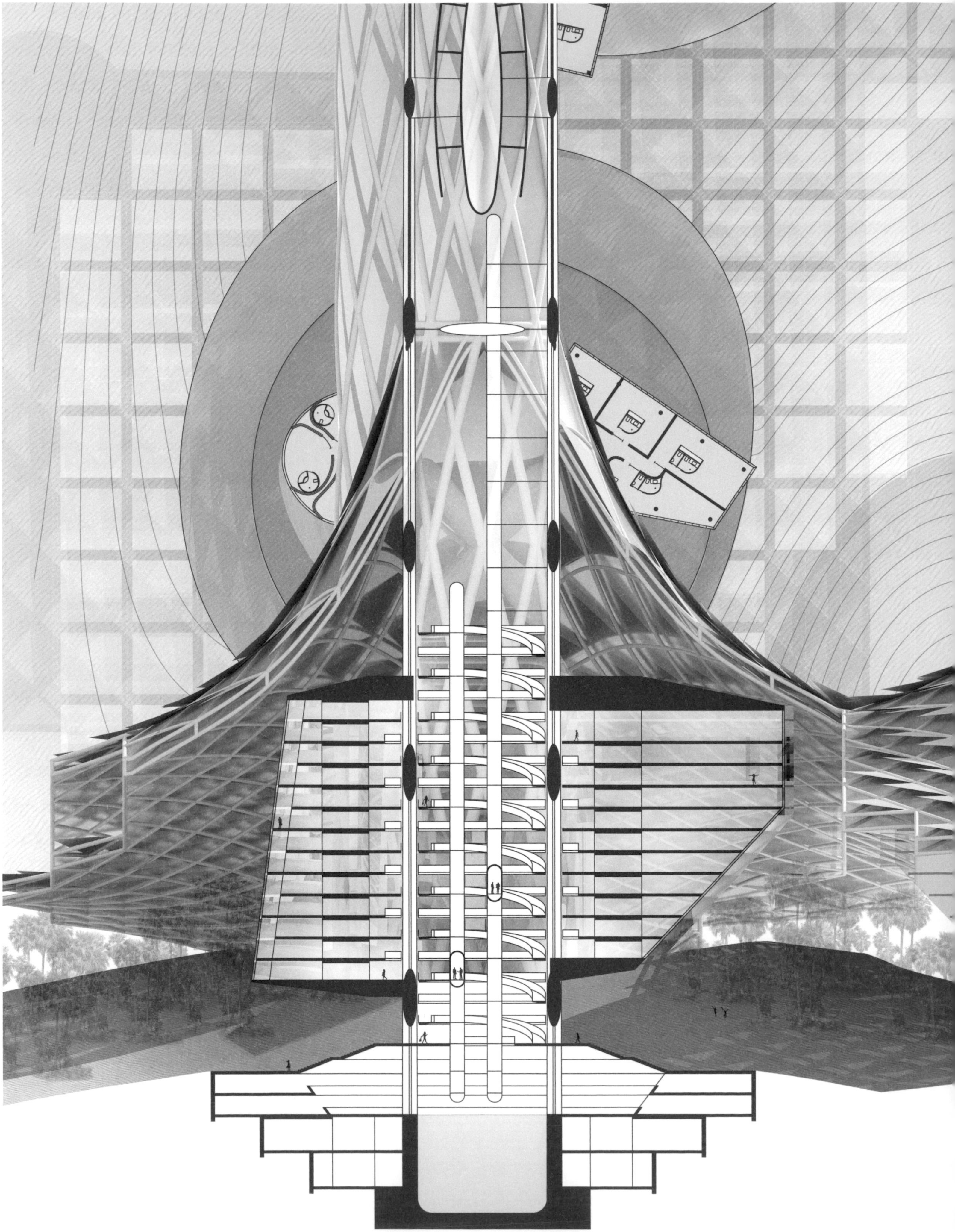

ASSIGNMENT

Faced with the overexploitation of inner and exterior regions of megacities, there are two forms of desertification today: the destruction of fertile land and the subsequent migration of populations suffering from it. More than two billion people live in arid regions of the globe. In that light, the project tries to offer and implement new sustainable solutions to global partners by stimulating new intellectual and economic movements within their regional populations while protecting their environments. ◣

LOCATION

This project is envisioned for the Eastern Sahara in Africa but can be easily applied to dry and hot areas around the globe from Southern California to the Middle East. ◣

CONCEPT

The Green Desert Mine envisions the transformation of hostile desert areas into fertile lands, rich with biodiversity and adapted to modern lifestyles, by fighting the green house effect with similar weapons. It is a design for a self-sufficient desert city clustered around the bases of huge thermal chimneys that are capable of recycling heat. ◣

ENERGY CONCEPT

After all, this grand architectural vision aims at obtaining an autonomous system in the form of a green mine where the symbolic riches unearthed are biodiversity. The updraft power plants described here are currently being developed by Schlaich Bergermann Solar. The first attempts to build an updraft power plant in Spain were undertaken in 1982. The difficulty of this construction lies in its huge size: the ideal chimney would be 1000 to 2000 metres high. ◣

REALISATION

Some 1400 citizens would be concentrated around the towers' superstructures. By stacking and elevating the city's functions and properties above ground, the footprint is limited to 1000 square metres, thus freeing the surrounding area to function as a garden. Sheltered by a translucent double membrane capable of collecting solar energy and transmitting it as thermal energy to the chimneys' turbines, the garden also functions as a mineral and biological filter system for the city's black water. Evaporated water is collected from the underside of the membrane and recycled. A drip irrigation system brings more water from nearby hills so that a rich and diverse biosphere can be encouraged alongside crops grown for food. ◣

01 View of the towers' superstructures.

INDEX

IMPRINT

ARCHITECTURE OF CHANGE 2

SUSTAINABILITY AND HUMANITY IN THE BUILT ENVIRONMENT

© Die Gestalten Verlag GmbH & Co. KG, Berlin 2009

For more information please check www.gestalten.com

Bibliographic information published by the Deutsche Nationalbibliothek. The Deutsche Nationalbibliothek lists this publication in the Deutsche Nationalbibliografie; detailed bibliographic data is available on the internet at http://dnb.d-nb.de.

None of the content in this book was published in exchange for payment by commercial parties or architects; Gestalten selected all included work based solely on its artistic merit.

This book was printed according to the internationally accepted FSC standards for environmental protection, which specify requirements for an environmental management system.

Mix
Produktgruppe aus vorbildlich bewirtschafteten Wäldern, kontrollierten Herkünften und Recyclingholz oder -fasern
www.fsc.org Zert.-Nr SGS-COC-003993
© 1996 Forest Stewardship Council
FSC

Gestalten is a climate neutral company and so are our products. We collaborate with the non-profit carbon offset provider myclimate (www.myclimate.org) to neutralize the company's carbon footprint produced through our worldwide business activities by investing in projects that reduce CO_2 emissions (www.gestalten.com/myclimate).

myclimate
Protect our planet

EDITED BY KRISTIN FEIREISS AND LUKAS FEIREISS

PREFACE BY KRISTIN FEIREISS

INTRODUCTION AND INTERVIEWS BY LUKAS FEIREISS

PROJECT DESCRIPTIONS BY LUKAS FEIREISS AND SOPHIE LOVELL

ART DIRECTION AND DESIGN BY BUREAU MARIO LOMBARDO, WWW.MARIOLOMBARDO.COM

COVER PHOTOGRAPHY BY IWAN BAAN

PROJECT MANAGEMENT BY JULIAN SORGE FOR GESTALTEN

PRODUCTION MANAGEMENT BY MARTIN BRETSCHNEIDER FOR GESTALTEN

PROOFREADING BY JOSEPH PEARSON

TRANSLATION PREFACE BY PATRICK SHEEHAN

TRANSLATION PETER SLOTERDIJK INTERVIEW BY STEVEN LINDBERG

PRINTED BY FREIBURGER GRAPHISCHE BETRIEBE GMBH & CO. KG, FREIBURG

MADE IN GERMANY

PUBLISHED BY GESTALTEN, BERLIN 2009

ISBN 978-3-89955-263-8

OLAFUR ELIASSON
360 rock series, 2006
9 C-prints, each 42 x 65 cm
Courtesy of the artist; Neugeriemschneider
Tanya Bonakdar Gallery, New York